Penn Greek Drama Series

Series Editors
David R. Slavitt
Palmer Bovie

The Penn Greek Drama Series presents fresh literary translations of the entire corpus of classical Greek drama: tragedies, comedies, and satyr plays. The only contemporary
series of all the surviving work of Aeschylus, Sophocles, Euripides, Aristophanes, and Menander, this collection brings
together men and women of literary distinction whose ver-
sions of the plays in contemporary English poetry can be
acted on the stage or in the individual reader's theater of the
mind.

The aim of the series is to make this cultural treasure acces-
sible, restoring as faithfully as possible the original luster of
the plays and offering in living verse a view of what talented
contemporary poets have seen in their readings of these
works so fundamental a part of Western civilization.

Aeschylus, 1: *The Oresteia*

Agamemnon, The Libation Bearers, The Eumenides

Edited and translated by
David R. Slavitt

PENN

University of Pennsylvania Press
Philadelphia

Copyright © 1998 University of Pennsylvania Press

Printed in the United States of America on acid-free paper

10 9 8 7 6 5 4 3 2 1

Published by
University of Pennsylvania Press
Philadelphia, Pennsylvania 19104-4011

Library of Congress Cataloging-in-Publication Data

Aeschylus.
[Works. English. 1997]
Aeschylus / edited by David R. Slavitt and Palmer Bovie
    p.   cm. — (Penn Greek drama series)
Contents: 1. The Oresteia
ISBN 0-8122-3416-2 (v. 1 : acid-free paper). — ISBN 0-8122-1627-X (pbk. :
v. 1 : acid free paper)
1. Aeschylus—Translations into English. 2. Greek drama (Tragedy)—
Translations into English. 3. Mythology, Greek—Drama. I. Slavitt, David R.,
1935-   . II. Bovie, Smith Palmer. III. Title. IV. Series.
PA3827.A657 1997
882'.01—dc21   97-28894
                                                                    CIP

For Deborah, Nadine, and Scott

Contents

Introduction

Palmer Bovie

Classical Greek tragedy, which flourished in Athens during the fifth century B.C., grew out of country festivals originating a century earlier. Three different celebrations in honor of Dionysus, known as the rural Dionysia, occurred during the winter months. One of these, the Lenaea, was also observed at Athens in the sanctuary of Dionysus. In addition to song it offered ecstatic dances and comedy. Another, the Anthesteria, lasted for three days as a carnival time of revelry and wine drinking. It also included a remembrance of the dead and was believed to be connected with Orestes' mythical return to Athens purged of guilt for killing his mother Clytemnestra.

The rural Dionysia were communal holidays observed to honor Dionysus, the god of wine, of growth and fertility, and of lightning. Free-spirited processions to an altar of Dionysus were crowned by lyrical odes to the god sung by large choruses of men and boys chanting responsively under the direction of their leader. The ritual included the sacrifice of a goat at the god's altar, from which the term "tragedy," meaning goat-song, may derive. Gradually themes of a more serious nature gained ground over the joyful, exuberant addresses to the liberating god, legends of familiar heroes, and mythological tales of divine retribution. But the undercurrent of the driving Dionysiac spirit was seldom absent, even in the sophisticated artistry of the masterful tragic poets of the fifth century.

Initially the musical texts were antiphonal exchanges between the chorus and its leader. Thespis, who won the prize of a goat for tragedy at Athens in 534 B.C., is traditionally said to have been the first to appear as an actor, separate from the chorus, speaking a prologue and making set speeches, with his face variously disguised by a linen mask. A fourth festival, the City Dionysia or the Great Dionysia, was instituted by the ruler Peisistratus, also in 534, and nine years later Aeschylus was born. It seems that the major era of Greek tragic art was destined to begin.

The Great Dionysia, an annual occasion for dramatic competitions in tragedy and comedy, was held in honor of Dionysus Eleutheros. Its five-day celebration began with a procession in which the statue of Dionysus was carried to the nearby village of Eleutherai (the site of the Eleusinian Mysteries) and then back, in a parade by torchlight, to Athens and the precincts of Dionysus on the lower slopes of the Acropolis. In the processional ranks were city officials, young men of military age leading a bull, foreign residents of Athens wearing scarlet robes, and participants in the dramatic contests, including the producers (*choregoi*), resplendent in colorful costumes. The ceremonies ended with the sacrificial slaughter of the bull and the installation of Dionysus' statue on his altar at the center of the orchestra.

For three days each of the poets chosen for the competition presented his work, three tragedies and one satyr play (a farcical comedy performed in the afternoon after an interval following the staging of tragedies). In the late afternoon comedies were offered. The other two days were marked by dithyrambic competitions, five boys' choruses on one day, five men's on the other. The dithyramb, earlier an excited dramatic dance, became in the Athenian phase a quieter performance, sung by a chorus of fifty and offering little movement.

The theater of Dionysus at Athens was an outdoor space on the southern slope of the Acropolis. A semicircular auditorium was created on the hillside from stone or marble slabs, or shaped from the natural rock with wooden seats added. Narrow stepways gave access to the seats, the front row of which could be fitted out with marble chairs for official or distinguished members of the audience. From sites visible today at Athens, Delphi, Epidaurus, and elsewhere, it is evident that the sloping amphitheater had excellent acoustic properties and that the voices of the actors and the chorus were readily heard.

The acting area began with an *orchestra*, a circular space some sixty feet in diameter where the chorus performed its dance movements, voiced its commentaries, and engaged in dialogue with the actors. In the center of the orchestra was an altar of Dionysus, and on it a statue of the god. Behind the orchestra several steps led to a stage platform in front of the *skene*, a wooden building with a central door and doors at each end and a flat roof. The actors could enter and exit through these doors or one of the sides, retiring to assume different masks and costumes for a change of role. They could also appear on the roof for special effects, as in Euripides' *Orestes* where at the end Orestes and Pylades appear, menacing Helen with death, before she is whisked away from them by Apollo. The skene's facade represented a palace or temple and could have an altar in front of it. Stage properties included the *eccyclema*, a wheeled platform that was rolled out from the central door or the side of the skene to display an interior setting or a tableau, as at the end of Aeschylus' *Agamemnon* where the murdered bodies of Agamemnon and Cassandra are proudly displayed by Clytemnestra.

Another piece of equipment occasionally brought into play was the *mechane*, a tall crane that could lift an actor or heavy objects (e.g., Medea in her chariot) high above the principals' heads. This device, also known as the *deus ex machina*, was favored by Euripides who, in the climactic scene of *Orestes* shows Apollo protecting Helen in the air high above Orestes and Pylades on the roof. Or a deity may appear above the stage to resolve a final conflict and bring the plot to a successful conclusion, as the figure of Athena does at the end of Euripides' *Iphigenia in Tauris*. Sections of background at each end of the stage could be revolved to indicate a change of scene. These *periaktoi*, triangular in shape, could be shown to the audience to indicate a change of place or, together with thunder and lightning machines, could announce the appearance of a god.

The actors wore masks that characterized their roles and could be changed offstage to allow one person to play several different parts in the same drama. In the earliest period tragedy was performed by only one actor in counterpoint with the chorus, as could be managed, for example, in Aeschylus' *Suppliants*. But Aeschylus himself introduced the role of a second actor, simultaneously present on the stage, Sophocles made use of a third, and he and Euripides probably a fourth. From such simple elements (the orchestra space for the chorus, the slightly raised stage and its scene front, the minimal cast of actors) was created the astonishingly powerful poetic drama of the fifth-century Athenian poets.

What we can read and see today is but a small fraction of the work produced by the three major poets and a host of fellow artists who presented plays in the dramatic competitions. Texts of tragedies of Aeschylus, Sophocles, and Euripides were copied and stored in public archives at Athens, along with Aristophanes' comedies. At some later point a selection was made of the surviving plays, seven by Aeschylus, seven by Sophocles, nine by Euripides, and ten others of his discovered by chance. In the late third and early second centuries B.C., this collection of thirty-three plays was conveyed to the great library of Alexandria, where scholarly commentaries, *scholia*, formed part of the canon, to be copied and transmitted to students and readers in the Greco-Roman cultural world.

Aeschylus (525–456 B.C.) was born of a noble Athenian family and lived during the early days of the city's democratic glory. Indeed, Pericles was the *choregus* (producer) of his *The Persians* in 472. Aeschylus was an honored, public-spirited citizen who fought in the infantry ranks at the battle of Marathon in 490 and ten years later at Salamis in the victorious struggles against the Persian invasions. His magnificent poetic style established the standard structure of high tragedy. There is the prologue, the opening chorus, the entrance of the actors, who engage in dialogue with their antagonists, with sympathetic friends, or with the chorus. The five or six episodes that constitute the narrative of the play's action are distinguished from one another by choral odes that reflect on the dilemmas arising from the plot or voice lyrical accounts of comparable situations known from myth or history.

The poetry does not refrain from vivid descriptions of death and disaster, but the actual scenes of violence occur offstage and are customarily reported by messengers entering with the shocking news. Greek tragedy, in general, is not the exploitation of human misfortune. It is, rather, a serious inquiry into moral problems, and at the outset Aeschylus equips his players and their choral spectators with challenging ideas. Revenge and retributive justice are misleading paths: "only the act of evil breeds other to follows"; "wisdom comes alone through suffering." Ares, the god of war, is the money changer of dead bodies who packs smooth urns with ashes that once were men: we are given such thoughts to ponder in the *Agamemnon*, but in the last play of this trilogy the court of the Areopagus frees Orestes of the guilt he incurred, with Electra's complicity, for matricide, and distributive justice prevails over an endless cycle of retaliation.

Prometheus the Titan, in *Prometheus Bound* chained in torment to a mountain rock for having brought the gift of fire to mortals and with it the basis of civilized progress, realizes that he has given humanity "blind hopes"; he admits that art (*techne*) is far weaker than necessity, human craft bound as it is by its own mortal limits. But as the two next plays in that trilogy suggest in their titles, *Prometheus Unbound* and *Prometheus the Firebearer*, his story ends in a triumphant reconciliation with Zeus, whose tyrannical pride has learned to replace selfish exclusiveness with an understanding of humankind's capability and right to improve their own condition.

Hermes, the messenger of Zeus in this cosmic drama, mocks Prometheus for having defied Zeus' authority and for being proud of enabling people to rise above their animal instincts and apply the use of reason. But, since Prometheus is to be released from bondage to the supreme ruler of the universe and ultimately recognized proudly(!) for giving mortals the means, the technology, for progress, the tragic ordeal becomes a triumph of good judgment. As George Orwell once wrote, somewhat bleakly, on the same subject: "Progress is not an illusion; but it is gradual and inevitably disappointing."[1]

Aeschylus' imagination ranges over the known world. His "suppliants," the fifty innocent Danaids, escape from Egypt and from their Egyptian cousins, who are menacing them with forced marriage, to Argos in Greece, where they gain the protection of the king, Pelasgus. The setting of *The Persians* is Susa, the residence of the Persian kings. Its characters include Atossa, the Queen Mother, and the ghost of Darius, and Xerxes, stripped of his pride. The drama is the only historical member of the canon, with its colorful description of the battle of Salamis and its poignant portrayal of an enemy in defeat. *The Seven Against Thebes* extends the revenge saga of the ruling dynasty of this city-state, even as it illustrates the utter futility of war.

Prometheus Bound is a cosmic pageant and a chance for Aeschylus to revel in his knowledge of geography. The wanderings of Io, foreseen by Prometheus (whose name means "forethought") describe the Near East, starting from the southern Caucasus and proceeding southward along the entire Ionian coast, to end in Egypt. In the course of this excursion through exotic place names, Aeschylus trained one sly glance on a river he himself invented. Prometheus warns Io not to cross the river Hybristes, the River

---

1. Orwell, "Politics and the English Language," *New Republic*, 1947; reprinted in various collections.

Pride. It tends to overflow its banks. One cannot locate this river on a map, but the idea sticks in one's mind. The whole drama is on a huge scale, its cast composed exclusively of immortals. We see Hephaestus and the huge figures Power and Force who hustle in as the play opens to bind the Titan to his mountain rock. He is visited and interviewed there by the Oceanids (who form the chorus) and their father Oceanus, then by Io who in her harassed state of prolonged wandering from Greece to Egypt will continue to be as tormented in her perpetual motion as Prometheus is tortured in his fixed bondage to the vindictive plans of Zeus. When Hermes arrives to try to talk Prometheus down and persuade him to compromise by divulging his secret knowledge of Zeus' future, Prometheus remains adamant in his defiance of tyrannical power. Their dialogue becomes a snarling duel of wits, as Hermes' tempting rationalizations try to offset Prometheus' naked truths. The play began with Prometheus being chained under the orders of Hephaestus, the god of fire, whose element he has dared to trespass upon. It ends with an earthquake and whirlwind that split the rock on which the hero has been impaled and hurl him into the abyss of Tartarus to endure further torment. An immortal cannot escape punishment by dying. We have witnessed the spectacle of sublime injustice. But from the further stages of the story as planned by Aeschylus it is apparent that the Titan, the benefactor of progress to mortals, outlasted his agonizing ordeal to become the object of mortals' grateful veneration.

The imagery and metaphorical insights of Aeschylus' verse range through a spectrum of associations. The Oceanids view Prometheus through "a mist of tears and fears"; they see him held "in bonds of adamantine shame." His words are sharpened swords. Fire is Hephaestus' flower, its flame a curling tendril. The want of good sense in Zeus has tangled him in a net of ruin. In *The Oresteia* Agamemnon's return is to "my palace for which I have so long yearned." Similar irony attends the chorus' description of him as a lion-king who leaped over the walls of Troy and lapped the blood of kings. Helen, whose name is cognate with the verb "to destroy," is Troy's "bride and bane." She is like a lion cub that grows up to develop claws and ferocity. Iphigenia is the innocent lamb of sacrifice. In ambiguous pleasure, Clytemnestra greets her husband's homecoming with "griefless heart," comparing him to "that brook from which [the parched and weakened traveler] can drink sweet water." She will be glad to slake her thirst.

In her turn, Electra says: "Even the dead can hope. Drowned men can rise like corks in the sea, and corpses ascend from their graves to thrive and prosper in the air, in their heirs who are yet alive."

In *The Eumenides* imagery is overshadowed by the strenuous rhetoric of argument, as the Furies lash out at Apollo and Athena, who engineer Orestes' trial and acquittal before a jury of twelve (the first in Athenian history). The drama explores Orestes' degree of responsibility for his wrongdoing and advances the idea that moral problems can be suitably addressed by the powers of human understanding. Crime is not something to be furious about but rather a complex social concern to be curious about. The spirit of vengeance symbolized by the Furies merely reinforces the human condition as the plight of a compulsive, aggressive creature. In effecting Orestes' redemption from sin Athena also works a magical transformation in the image of the Erinyes, the Furies, who are persuaded to assume a new role as the Eumenides, kindly spirits. They will reside in Athens as guardian spirits, gladly responsible for the protection of social justice among its citizens. The surprising transformation fulfills the hope expressed much earlier in the trilogy by a choral refrain in the *Agamemnon*:

We sing a dirge but hope that good may prevail.

The Oresteia

Translated by
David R. Slavitt

Translator's Preface

Most of what I want to say about Aeschylus and *The Oresteia* is in the text—or ought to be. A translation of a great work is not so much a rendition into a different language as the record of a reading. It is the outcome of a literary encounter, an act of criticism and interpretation, and even, under ideal circumstances, an exploration not only of the text but of the translator's soul. Each work of literature, then, as it resonates in the hearts and minds of its audience, elicits a response that is novel, individual, unprecedented—just as the experience and character and even the neural connections of each member of that audience are unprecedented and unique.

Still, a few remarks may not be altogether out of order. It is certainly appropriate to mention that Aeschylus was born in 528 or 527 B.C., that his first play was probably staged in 499, that he fought the Persians at Marathon in the famous battle of 490 (in which his brother Cynegeiros was killed), and that he probably fought at Salamis and Plataia in 480. Pericles himself financed the production of *The Persians* (472), which was a part of the trilogy that won the drama prize that year. With *The Oresteia*, the only complete trilogy to survive from the Greek tragedians, Aeschylus won first prize in 458, for the eighteenth and last time. He died in 456 at Gela, in Sicily.

And about the play? It is surely the most influential and arguably still the best dramatic work ever written. As we enter a new millennium, it is chastening to think that literature runs downhill—from the Bible and from Homer and Aeschylus. The Bible, of course, is not merely a work of literature—but neither are the Homeric epics or the Greek tragedies in which the rituals of religious observance were only beginning their gradual devolution into what we would recognize as secular theatrical productions. When the gods speak in these plays, they do so not merely in an interesting if antique literary convention but in as lively and direct a way as the Lord

spoke to Abraham or Moses or Job. The choruses in Greek tragedy serve as
representatives of the community in a way that is mostly unfamiliar to us
now except in the exercise of congregational prayer.

The Oresteia was performed, after all, at the Great Dionysia, an annual
festival that lasted for five days. This religious celebration was funded and
administered by the *polis* in the ninth month of the calendar year (for us, it
would be, roughly, March). On the first day there would be a *proagon*, a
procession and a sacrifice of bulls that ended in a great feast (the Greeks
rarely ate meat except on festival occasions), and a competition of men's
and boys' choruses. On the next three days, each of the three tragedians
who had been selected to compete would present three tragedies and a satyr
play to an audience of as many as fourteen thousand people in an outdoor
theater half the size of a modern football stadium. The tragedies could be
connected, as they are in *The Oresteia*, or they could be on three separate
topics. Before the presentation of the dramas there would be a sacrifice and
a libation poured by the ten most important military and political officials
of the state. Announcements were made of the citizens who had benefited
the *polis* and who were awarded honorific crowns. Young men whose fathers
had died fighting for the *polis*—orphans who were supported by the state
and educated at public expense—would parade in armor that had been pro-
vided for them and would publicly affirm that they were now ready to take
their fathers' places in the military service. Then, on the fifth, day, five
comedies would be presented. An assembly was held in the theater two days
after the festival in which the merits of the different plays were debated and
prizes awarded to the playwrights and actors. Think of this full spectacle as
a theater festival that also combined features of Memorial Day, Veterans'
Day, the Fourth of July, Christmas, and Oscar night.

About the trilogy itself, I am reluctant to say much. The scholarship and
the body of critical writing about *The Oresteia* is large and not difficult to
find. For those who are reading the play for the first time, though, I might
point out a few things to consider along the way. First of all, there is the
tension between Agamemnon's public responsibilities and his duty as the
head of a family. As the leader of the Achaeans at Aulis, he is told by
the priest that he must sacrifice his daughter Iphigenia in order to propitiate
the gods and get the winds to shift so the armada can put to sea. He is the

general and a king, and this is clearly his duty. But as a father, it is just as clearly his duty to protect his daughter. Tragedy is not a struggle between good and evil but a contest between two mutually exclusive goods. Unlike Abraham, Agamemnon has no angel who appears at the critical moment offering a ram he can use as a substitute for the child. Agamemnon is forced to choose, knowing perfectly well that either option is terrible.

Agamemnon kills Iphigenia; Clytemnestra then kills Agamemnon; Orestes then kills Clytemnestra. This alternation of genders is significant and leads ultimately to the resolution in which Athena intervenes—a female who is nonetheless male-like, virginal, a warrior goddess. In the argument between the Furies (female) and Apollo (male) about what should happen to Orestes, Athena is as close as possible to being neutral, if not neuter, and disinterested. Because she is also the patroness of Athens, the dramatist's homage to her in the denouement is an expression of patriotic (and matriotic) pride.

These issues are all present, in the background. Downstage, the characters are struggling with other, perhaps more immediate concerns. Are the lives we lead our own or are we merely the toys of the gods? We believe, most of us, in reason and justice, but we recognize limits beyond which those concepts cannot take us. Can there be a different kind of justice, in which bloodguilt passes from generation to generation? To what degree is the behavior of Agamemnon, or Clytemnestra, or Electra and Orestes predetermined for them?

Those are the great questions. Discuss. Write for an hour. Compare and contrast. As if literature were a series of hoops for young people to jump through.

I'd rather talk about the ways my version differs from others. Translating a play is an intimate experience, and the translator is forced to look closely at every line of each speech, each moment in the drama, each beat, as they say. At that very tight focal length, there are discoveries, small but precious surprises. One must make emotional sense of what is on the page in order to find the right tone and cadence in English. Or, if not right, then at least plausible, emotionally and intellectually possible.

My main discovery, I think, was that Aeschylus is often funnier than I remembered or than any of my guides would have led me to expect. There is a scene in *Agamemnon* in which the king is killed offstage while the chorus dithers, wondering what those shouts might mean. That goes beyond dramatic irony to willful stupidity—and humor, although we cannot quite laugh out loud. The tone is bizarre and surprising, as is the porter's scene in *Macbeth* with the knocking at the gate. Both, I think, are strategies that turn away from the poetry of language to rely on sheer dramatization. We know, in *Macbeth*, what has just happened, and that is so large and burdensome a piece of knowledge as to transform the most ordinary piece of business— like the knocking at the gate—into the detail of a nightmare. In *Agamemnon*, it is happening *now*, and we who know perfectly well what is going on are unable to do or say anything. Such knowledge is unspeakable, and the inability of the chorus to speak is both comical and awesome. (I have allowed myself a little freedom with the language of this scene in order to let what I see as the emotional and dramatic color of the transaction come through to the reader and the audience. My choice, frankly, was between this and utter incomprehensibility.)

The unspeakable in Aeschylus is important, and in it he finds a peculiarly powerful dramatic device, for at the heart of these plays there are protracted silences. In *Agamemnon*, Cassandra arrives with the king in his chariot to be welcomed by Clytemnestra and the chorus. As Bernard Knox observes in "Aeschylus and the Third Actor," Cassandra's

> name is not pronounced, her presence not explained, not even mentioned, as she sits there silent through the long dramatic confrontation, through Agamemnon's haughty and insensitive speech of greeting, through Clytemnestra's baleful speech of welcome, overloaded with flattering superlatives and laced with threatening ambiguities, through the tussle of wills between husband and wife which ends in the wife's victory and Agamemnon's consent to enter the palace treading on the blood-red carpet she has spread for him.[1]

Agamemnon explains to Clytemnestra and the audience that this is his concubine, but the Trojan woman keeps silent. Clytemnestra offers a final

---

1. Bernard M. W. Knox, *Word and Action: Essays on the Ancient Theater* (Baltimore: Johns Hopkins University Press, 1979), pp. 42–43.

prayer before following her husband into the palace to murder him, but still Cassandra holds her peace. Then Clytemnestra returns to order Cassandra inside, and this is the first time that even the name of the figure in the chariot has been spoken. There follows a scene between the two in which Clytemnestra urges, threatens, but Cassandra makes no reply, no sign of understanding. Perhaps she is deaf and dumb, as Clytemnestra suggests. Does she know Greek? (Or, in the audience, we may wonder whether she is perhaps a nonspeaking actor.) After Clytemnestra goes back inside, the chorus urges Cassandra to be sensible and follow the queen. "And suddenly," Knox remarks, "just as we begin to think that she will never speak, she does. Or rather she screams. '*Otototi popoi da.*' It is a formulaic cry of grief and terror, one of those cries ancient Greek is so rich in, no words at all but merely syllables, which express emotion no words could adequately convey."

In *The Libation Bearers* we have another dramatic silence that is broken at a critical moment, for Pylades, Orestes' companion, just stands there for the longest time without a word. Then, when he does speak, he has only three lines. But they are critical lines in which he reminds the hesitating Orestes that what is now at risk is the truth of Apollo's oracles and the sworn pledge of faith.

It is as if there were, on the one side, the torrents of eloquence from the characters and the chorus, and, in opposition somehow, these great silences. Perhaps I am aware of them because I did not have to worry about translating them properly but could rely on them to speak for themselves. Cassandra's syllables remain as they were, on the boundary between speech and silence, a holy cry that is wholly a cry: *Otototi popoi da.*

It is all there is to say when there is nothing to say.

Agamemnon

Cast

SENTRY
CHORUS of elders of Argos
CLYTEMNESTRA, wife of Agamemnon
HERALD
AGAMEMNON, king of Mycenae
CASSANDRA, daughter of Priam, king of Troy, and
    Agamemnon's captive
AEGISTHUS, king of Argos, Clytemnestra's lover
NONSPEAKING
    Attendants of Clytemnestra, Agamemnon, Aegisthus

(On a watchtower of the citadel of Agamemnon in Argos.)

SENTRY
    A long watch. It has been years now of peering
    into this blackness. High on the citadel tower,
    my eyes fixed on the sky's blank slate, I wait
    and pray for a sign, a discernible gleam. I stare
    at nothing. A dog's life! Chained up, I can feel
    that single sharp bark, a lump in my throat
    I shall, in time, cough out.
                        Meanwhile the lofty
    stars overhead spin in contempt or, worse,
    in unconcern, as the seasons they signal come
    and go and the wind blows hot or cold.
                        Either way,   10
    I'm stuck here, black behind me, a deeper black
    out there, until the spark of that signal fire
    shows red as blood or the flames raging at Troy.
        She commands it, whose strength of will is such
    that, if she were not queen, she would be our tyrant.

At the thought of her narrowed eyes, my own grow wide
in fear that sleep would close. I stamp my feet
through the long night, or sometimes sing or recite—
anything to keep awake. Or weep
at the fate of our royal house with its dire troubles,   20
the price, sometimes, of grandeur.

                    Every moment
is an unendurable knife edge, but all together
they stretch out making a plane of time . . . I pray
for that signal of my release from this hard duty
to flash out in the indifferent heavens.

                              Now?

(The signal fire flashes.)

Is it? Can prayers at last be answered? Yes!
The blaze of truth! The light at the end of the night
that breaks as we were about to despair. Rejoice,
and dance the dance of thanksgiving.

                         Ho, there! Ho!
Let the queen be summoned. Rouse her from bed   30
and bid her light the torches of joy that gleaming
light in the distance kindles. Sing and dance,
for Troy is taken. We are at peace!

                        A long
watch it was, but it's over. The master comes
bringing us the richest gift of his triumph,
the miracle of ordinary days.

(A slight pause, as his mood changes.)

Words fail. Like a dumb beast I will stare
at his face and kiss his hand.

                     What can we say,
any of us who have lived to see this day,
of the troubles of his house?

                        Not a single word!   40

(He descends. Below, the Chorus of Argive Elders files in.)

CHORUS
    Ten years ago, against the might of Priam
    the sons of Atreus set forth
    under one banner,
    by the grace of Zeus,
    with their thousand ships
    Agamemnon and Menelaus,
    joined in honor.

    The scream of angry eagles tore the sky,
    who wheeled and soared overhead
    on powerful wings   50
    above a plundered
    nest. For a lost
    chick, they grieved.
    Such was the hurt and rage
    of these two kings.

    Could the gods ignore that child-avenging cry?
    Apollo or Pan or even Zeus
    Xenios who rules
    in heaven, heard
    and loosed our host   60
    against the Trojans
    to fetch her home,
    at the cost of much clotted blood
    in those tidal pools

    beneath their fortress walls, that connoisseur
    of husbands. Three times mated, she
    was Sparta's queen,
    then concubine
    to Paris, then
    to Deiphobus, his brother.   70
    Truly obscene,

can the stain of it be washed away somehow
by the shedding of blood and tears?
At grievous price
the expedition
commenced, and now
is the ritual yet complete
of sacrifice?

We who were too old to go to war,
we who remained at home,   80
had nothing but canes
that we could brandish
in heaven's face before
these palace gates in protest.
Our fear remains

undiminished. Like children, we overheard
the frightening sounds of the grown-ups' quarrels.
They reconciled,
but we were afraid
of what we inferred   90
from Clytemnestra's demeanor
in grief for her child.

How can we celebrate now, and how can our hearts
soar as the flames leap up from the altars
of the city's gods?
We hope for the best
but fear the worst,
as we guess what the fates have in store
and figure the odds.

FIRST CHORISTER

But let us chant a victory ode together,   100
together having endured the trials of the years.
May our faith in the gods inspire us to sing
convincingly of this triumph. As sons of Hellas

rose up in vengeance for our dishonored king,
those two ominous birds
soared overhead to the right,
one with a black tail and one with a white.
We stared up and there,
in their talons, they held a pregnant hare.
With what, we asked, was that moment pregnant?   110

CHORUS
    We sing a dirge but hope that good may prevail.

FIRST CHORISTER
    The prophet spoke, interpreting for us the signs
    of heaven's intent. Those birds were our two kings,
    the sons of Atreus' house, and that hare, their prey,
    was time, he said, "in the fullness of which Priam's city
    shall surely fall, and none shall get away,
    if only the gods permit,
    for Artemis cannot approve
    the death of one of her creatures, and her love
    we must contrive to earn."   120
    As we heard him speak those words, our concern
    grew. With what was the moment pregnant?

CHORUS
    We sing a dirge but hope that good may prevail.

FIRST CHORISTER
    "Apollo," he prayed, "hear me and intercede
    with your sister, Artemis, lovely and tender-hearted,
    that she not take offense and resolve therefore to oppose
    the Greeks in our purpose. Our strength in arms is great
    as mortals reckon, but nothing at all to those
    of the winds and the waves. We need,
    no matter how great the cost,   130
    the help of the gods, without which we are lost.
    Our prayers we must try to make good

by the sacrifice of human, of royal, blood."
With what were the words of Calchas pregnant?

CHORUS

We sing a dirge but hope that good may prevail.

SECOND CHORISTER

Whoever, whatever he is, we will, if it please him,
address him as Zeus, a name we speak in awe,
knowing he takes the measure of each of our hearts
from greatest to least. Uranus, Cronus saw
his triumph end their glory, and wisdom starts   140
with prayer to Zeus, the master of heaven and earth,

whose difficult course of instruction to men is severe.
But, surely, whatever we know, we must admit
we learn from our pain. Through tears, then, let us praise
almighty Zeus, who has inflicted it
but given us solace, too, at the ends of our days,
when we may dream of grace, of peace and plenty.

FIRST CHORISTER

And Agamemnon, the fleet commander, heard
the soothsayer's declaration, but said not a word
of blame or reproach to Calchas, looking instead   150
to the skies and the seas to confirm what the priest had said.
The winds were strong
but all from the wrong
direction, onshore at Aulis where they lay
waiting, waiting, but the winds would not relent.
And the priest said again, more clearly, what he had meant,

at which time the king spoke up. He swallowed his grief
and said, "It is bitter, bitter, being the chief.
To slay my own little girl? With my hand to pour

her virgin's blood on an altar to go to war?   160
And yet, if I fail
we never shall sail
to Troy, as we have pledged to each other to do,
and I shall dishonor myself and each of you."

CHORUS

What is a man to do? This unspeakable thing
they spoke of, an offense, an outrage, unholy,
and wrong, wrong,
as every bone in his body knew, and nerve.

Necessity, Goddess Ananke, dictates to a king,
and he obeys, albeit reluctantly, slowly.   170
He makes his heart strong
and does what he must, having been called to serve.

FIRST CHORISTER

"Father," the princess cries, "Father,
save me!"
Would that he could.
At her keening, his heart breaks and his eyes
stream tears
that do them no good.

He bids the attendants dress her; he nods;
they raise her   180
high for the kill
like a lamb or a kid on the altar. Her screaming
is smothered:
they hold her mouth still.

Her eyes, nevertheless, are flashing
in terror,
outrage, and blame,

and strike into each man's pitying heart
a dagger
poisoned with shame.   190

CHORUS

What happened then, we did not see.
The eyes, the brain,
turn away at such events.
For wisdom that the gods dole out
we pay in pain
that we hope, at last, relents

as the dawn comes with its wan light
to offer relief
from dreams we could scarcely bear,
sordid, horrid, shameful, woeful,   200
and so full of grief
that even the brave despair.
(Clytemnestra enters.)

SECOND CHORISTER

That light now breaks, and we await the day's
outcome in hope that, somehow, all will be well.
Our fears may be great, but she whom we all praise
as close to our lord has preserved the citadel.

FIRST CHORISTER

You have summoned us here, Clytemnestra, and we obey
gladly and pay you reverence, consort to our king.
Is it good news or bad? We wait for you to say,
who will show us the way to accept what fate may bring.   210

CLYTEMNESTRA

As the proverb has it, the dawn is born
of Mother Night, and I bring the happy news
that the Argives have taken Troy.

FIRST CHORISTER
Can we trust our ears and believe in such longed-for words?

CLYTEMNESTRA
Believe me. I say that Troy is destroyed. It's true.

FIRST CHORISTER
Tears of joy well up in my eyes.

CLYTEMNESTRA
Those tears proclaim your heart's allegiance.

FIRST CHORISTER
How comes this report? Are you sure of your source, my lady?

CLYTEMNESTRA
If anything is real, then this is real.

SECOND CHORISTER
Dreams sometimes seem real. We all have dreamt . . .   220

CLYTEMNESTRA
It is no dream. We are awake. Believe it!

FIRST CHORISTER
But rumors are sometimes attractive. We wish to believe!

CLYTEMNESTRA
Do not presume. I am neither a child nor a fool.

SECOND CHORISTER
What time of day was it when Troy was destroyed?

CLYTEMNESTRA
Not day, but at night. Last night, in fact.

FIRST CHORISTER
    And the news has arrived already? How could that happen?

CLYTEMNESTRA
    At the speed of light. Hephaestus' sacred fire
    blazed from beacon tower to beacon tower,
    from Ida's top to Lemnos, and from there to Athos,
    that island sacred to Zeus, where they set the blaze   230
    they had kept prepared so long, and the tongues of flame
    leaped up in the dark night in a kind of chorus
    singing the victory hymn in splendid crescendo.
    From point to point in the sky, as if the sun
    had prematurely risen, the rays of light
    dazzled the eyes of the sentries, who in their joy
    touched torch to waiting tinder. At Euripus' shore
    they signaled from Euboea across the strait
    to their cohorts alert on the Boeotian headland
    who repeated the exercise, and the flames took hold   240
    of the heaped-up heather to flare as their gladness flared,
    and those on station across the plain on Cithaeron
    saw it redden the sky. Relieved, overjoyed
    after all those years of waiting, they lit their fire
    to pass the message onward. Across the water
    on Aigiplanctus' slopes they saw and forthwith
    bearded the heavens with flames, and so on down
    to the bluffs on the Saronic narrows at the gulf
    they call Engia, and here on the Peloponnese
    they lit yet another blaze the watchman on post   250
    on the peak of Arachneus saw. He set
    the last of the signal fires, the one our man
    on the citadel roof could see, in direct descent
    from its forebear on distant Ida that even now
    has not yet burned away. Its heat and light
    have, by such leaps and bounds along the race-course
    we laid out long ago, arrived in an instant,
    as quick as thinking. And do you doubt me now?

FIRST CHORISTER

    Lady, I cannot. Almost mute with amazement,
    it is all I can do to offer my prayers of thanks   260
    to the gods, as I shall do forthwith. But tell me,
    in more detail, whatever else you may know.

CLYTEMNESTRA

    Troy, as I say, is today in Achaean hands
    and within those walls are ill-assorted noises
    that dislike coming together, as the vinegar does
    with oil in the mixing bowl: the sobs of the vanquished
    and shouts of joy of the victors, the keening of women
    and guffaws of happy men. The scene is bleak
    with corpses of Trojan soldiers piling up in the streets
    and wives and mothers and daughters, still alive,   270
    wailing the griefs of slaves over their loved ones'
    careless bodies. The Greeks, meanwhile, make merry,
    the world their buffet, with riches and dainties on offer
    everywhere to consume or waste, like gods
    as free for the time with the city as they, the immortals,
    are with the world. Each man has drawn by lot
    a billet, no longer a tent or the frosty sky,
    but a roof overhead, and perhaps a couch with pillows
    on which to sprawl at his ease, the master now
    of whatever his eye may light on, to drowse and dream   280
    of phantom horrors from which he can free himself
    at will any time, blinking and rubbing his eyes.
        This liberty, I trust, may not extend
    to a license to desecrate the city's shrines
    or offend its gods from whose dread reach no man
    can think himself secure. The voyage home
    they know involves some risk. I pray the thrill
    of this moment of their triumph may not make them
    mad—to rape and plunder and carry on,
    not as men but as beasts in rut and frenzy.   290
    Let them be wary, and let the good prevail,

that our husbands and sons may be repaid with good
whose need for the gods' favor can never end.
What I know as a woman, I fear men may forget.

SECOND CHORISTER

Any man of prudence would surely agree and endorse
what you have here pronounced. For our part, we
offer prayers of thanks to heaven's gods
that we have at last, and at great expense, succeeded.
(Clytemnestra exits.)

FIRST CHORISTER

Lord Zeus, we address you with reverence, and you, sweet Night,
who have brought us these great tidings of grace and glory.   300
Yours was the wide-spread net that ensnared the Trojans,
trapping them all, the old and the young, in its doom.
Zeus Xenios, the lord of host and guest,
we worship you in your justice and power blessed.

Yours was the bow. You stretched it long ago,
and your deadly arrow has found its target at last—
Paris and all the house of Priam. Troy
was wrong to ignore and to flout your just precepts.
The arrowhead flew neither long nor short nor wide
of the mark, and this is the death of Trojan pride.   310

SECOND CHORISTER

Lord Zeus it was whose blow destroyed the Trojans.
We can see it, plain as a lightning bolt from the sky
that flashes divine displeasure. Whosoever offends
in the world below, those who ignore or defy
the sanctities of the gods, will assuredly die.
Men should aspire to virtue for its own sake.
But a sinner's fear of the gods can also make
for a life that is not without worth
for mortals who tread the earth.

The fall of the mighty who violate the laws   320
the gods have imposed is awesome. If, in their pride,
they transgress against the gods and invite the reproof
of mighty woes, then which of us can hide
his wicked thoughts and deeds? Let us decide
that in modesty, prudence, and circumspection we
may avoid such retribution as we can see
destroying those men who do
whatever they're tempted to.

FIRST CHORISTER

Lord Zeus, we think we are free
to do as we please, but we find   330
that wickedness can cost
the earth, and they are lost
who run after pleasure as children
on the grass chase winged birds.

The gods are deaf to the prayers
such people may frame: they bring
ruin to all their kin
and townsfolk by their sin
with the gods' relentless correction,
awesome beyond all words.   340

SECOND CHORISTER

Such a man was Paris,
who came as a guest
to the house of the sons of Atreus.
The gods detest
a man who steals the wife
of his host and ruins his life.

Helen's beauty could dazzle
men who would see
quickly enough the carnage

of warfare, for she   350
brought dishonor to men. Her name
is a synonym now for shame.

FIRST CHORISTER
    "Woe," the seers cried out,
    "woe for the house and its master!
    Woe for the marriage bed on which he lies alone,
    yearning." In this disaster,
    beauty itself turns hateful
    and ugly to him. Oh, shout
    the pity of it, the woe!
    In his dreams, he sees her face   360
    teasing him, beckoning,
    taunting . . . He reaches out but she is gone.
    His grief is past reckoning.
    The princes of other cities
    imagine themselves in his place
    and share his deep chagrin.

SECOND CHORISTER
    The god of war keeps a shop
    where he deals out portions of glory
    for measures of blood and tears.
    The weights in his scales are corpses   370
    and urns of ashes, the crop
    of the battlefields of the earth.

    The heroes of Argos, brave
    in battle, are stricken. They fall,
    and comrades mourn their deaths . . .
    For another man's wife? Who goes
    for a reason like that to his grave?
    What's a king's honor worth?

FIRST CHORISTER
　　Such subversive talk, once it gets going,
　　is dangerous, as kings know all too well,   380
　　as if the Furies were eager to teach the lesson
　　of modesty to men, whose heads can swell
　　and bring them down. The trees on the mountaintop
　　are the ones that bolts of lightning are likely to lop.

SECOND CHORISTER
　　Such worries are not for the likes of us. I am glad
　　not to be great, or rich, or powerful, and not
　　to be envied by anyone. Perhaps this news is true,
　　and the war is won they went to Troy and fought
　　for honor and wealth. I pray that it may prove true,
　　or else who knows what we shall suffer through?   390

THIRD CHORISTER
　　If it's only a rumor, we're no worse off than before.

SECOND CHORISTER
　　But how can the women endure more months of the war?

THIRD CHORISTER
　　I fear, therefore, the rumors women retail,
　　even this woman . . .

FIRST CHORISTER
　　　　　　　　　　　We shall soon enough know if this story
　　of flashing beacon fires on mountaintops
　　be true or merely a dream. But look, a herald
　　approaches, bearing the olive branch of his office.
　　His clothes are covered with thirsty dust, the mud's drier
　　sister . . .

THIRD CHORISTER
  I beg your pardon? This is no time
  for display of rhetorical figures.

FIRST CHORISTER
                      What else can we do   400
  until he gets here? How better pass the painful
  interval, as we pray for some confirmation
  of what we have dared to allow ourselves to hope?
  We shall know better or worse.

SECOND CHORISTER
                      If common prayer
  has any weight with the gods, the news will be good,
  for surely we are combined in fervent purpose.
  (A herald enters.)

HERALD
  I greet my Argive fatherland. Ten years
  I have dreamed of this happy day when I once again
  could walk on this earth where I was born, come back
  to live here, die here, and be buried here.   410
  I bless this place, its air, its light, and its gods.
  May Zeus send down upon us no more bolts
  of anger, such as we saw at the walls of Troy.
  And lord Apollo, and you, my patron Hermes,
  the herald of all heralds, I pray you all
  receive in grace those of us now returning,
  survivors of the battlefield and its trials,
  who will look with joy at these palace walls, these roofs,
  these statues of all the gods that face the sunrise.
  The silent stones glow in welcome and dance   420
  in our grateful, glistening eyes as we look upon them,
  a sight restored as if to the blind. We bring
  our king Agamemnon home. As is right and proper,
  greet him in gladness, for he has conquered Troy,

has dug out that rank weed with Zeus' mattock,
himself a tool of the god, too. That ground
is cleared. Their altars and shrines are all torn down.
No stone stands on another stone in a ruin
that is absolute. On Troy's stiff neck our king
has placed the heavy yoke of the slave. In triumph   430
Atreus' son comes home, a happy man,
worthy beyond all mortal men of praise
and reverence. His great vengeance has blotted out
the crime by which the Trojan prince began
this bloody war. Paris took Helen home.
But she is back; Paris is dead; and that home
is a mound of ashes.

FIRST CHORISTER
                      We greet you, Achaean herald,
    in gladness.

HERALD
    If the gods were to summon me now, I am content,
    having lived to see this moment.

FIRST CHORISTER
                          What you yearned for,   440
    we all desired, even to desperation.

HERALD
    Despair? How so? Had you need of your prince's protection?
    Against what danger?

FIRST CHORISTER
                  Some things, we have learned, it is better
    neither to speak nor even think of. Silence,
    even that of the grave, can be anodyne.

HERALD

But the dangers now are past, and years of waiting
at last are ended. They were not without their cost,
but which of us can expect a painless passage
like that of a god? The lot of mortals is hard.
We were content to survive each day's new trials,   450
the voyage out, cramped in those floundering boats,
the difficult landing, the labor of pitching our camp
in bad weather, our verminous clothing soaked,
and then the cold that froze the birds in the skies.
It's a vile place! Freezing in winter and hot,
oppressively hot, in the summer. You can feel
your eyeballs poach in your head. And then, the fighting . . .
But it's over now, and the living will tell the stories
of hardships we all endured. The dead don't care,
but even they would approve our boast that the Greek   460
host has triumphed. We took them down, those Trojans,
and now that we're back, we can nail up the trophies of war
in the shrines of the gods in gratitude and praise.
Whoever sees these spoils in the holy temples
will know how once in Hellas there were fighters
unrivaled in all the world, great cities' leaders
and a host of men of valor, and bless them all.
For what they have done, let all of us here be grateful
now and forever—I've nothing more to say.

FIRST CHORISTER

So much for my doubts. It is good, sometimes, to be wrong.   470
These are excellent tidings. Thus should the young men always
correct their doubting elders. I shall watch with interest
as Clytemnestra reacts to this herald's news.
(*Clytemnestra enters.*)

CLYTEMNESTRA

You hear? You see with your own eyes? On a woman
who might be misled, you men could not rely!
Where are they now who scorned my beacon-fires

or feared that my woman's heart might have swayed
                my judgment?
Silent, they study their feet and try to forget
their pompous postures as men-of-the-world, too grand
to pay any heed to a mere woman's hysterics.   480
I have performed my sacrifice, giving thanks
to the great gods; I urge them now to do likewise.
Those details the herald brings I do not need,
for I shall soon enough hear from the king's own mouth
the story of this long war. I must go to prepare
a loving wife's welcome. My lord returns,
and nothing is sweeter in any woman's eyes
than to open the door to him whom the gods have spared
and brought home safe. Tell the king I await him,
a loyal and faithful wife, his household's mistress,   490
and the foe of all his foes. Bid him make haste
to his country's and his wife's arms open wide
in eagerness and love to welcome him home.
(Clytemnestra exits)

HERALD

    What better words could any wife pronounce?
    What better truths could any husband hear?

FIRST CHORISTER

    They gleam like new-minted coins, but ring on the counter
    in a way that's not quite right. But, Herald, tell us,
    what news of Menelaus? Has he returned
    safe on his homeward voyage? All has gone well?

HERALD

    What would I give to be able to tell you truly   500
    how we may be at ease on his account!

SECOND CHORISTER

    Another burden to bear? A new disaster?

HERALD
Who knows for sure? The truth of it is that his ship
was swept away, lost to the rest of the fleet.

SECOND CHORISTER
How did it happen? A sudden storm at sea?

HERALD
Your guess has hit truth's target. That's just what happened.

SECOND CHORISTER
Has anyone heard any more? Where there any survivors?

HERALD
None but the all-seeing eye of the sun in heaven
saw what occurred.

SECOND CHORISTER
               Tell us about that storm.

HERALD
This is a day of joy we should not spoil   510
with stories of dreadful events. How can we thank
the Olympian gods at the same time as we feed
the appetite of the Furies for mortals' griefs?
How shall I mix the joy and the woe together?
Should the city rejoice, while here and there the eyes
of mourners look on in their doubled pain that Ares
with his double-plaited lash so loves? It's cruel—
as it was cruel at sea, where the waves came up
to wash our triumphs away. Fire and water together,
those implacable foes, united to harass our ships   520
and scatter our flotilla every which way.
We were off the coast of Thrace, in lightning and thunder
with a pelting rain coming down, and in garish tableaux
we could see the damage, and then were left to imagine

how our companions struggled and hope they survived
from moment to moment and breath to hard-fought breath
of blessed air. At dawn, when it eased, we could see
in the first light what we'd never thought to behold—
that our ship had survived unscathed, its hull, its mast,
its rigging still intact, and we thanked the gods   530
for yet again having spared us. But how they fared
in the other boats we could not begin to suppose.
We remembered the mountainous waves that could well
                    have swamped
their pitching and yawing vessels. We saw the shore
and the black rocks on which they might have been driven,
but nothing else save the blue of the sky and the empty
blue of the sea. At least there were no wrecked ships,
no flotsam . . . We could cling to our hopes. We mumbled
long-odds prayers that somehow they might have been spared.
We had survived. Perhaps they had also been lucky.   540
Menelaus is strong and shrewd, the kind of man
one never writes off. What can we do but hope
that the will of Zeus is not so adverse to men
that he could allow catastrophe to strike
in such a way and at such a time? You know
as much as I know now, good sirs, believe me.
(Herald exits.)

CHORUS
    The name of Helen fouls the mouth,
    a curse. How did the fates arrange
    that so uncanny cognomen
    she bore?   550

FIRST CHORISTER
    Helen, destroyer: *Helenaus*, destroyer of ships;
    Heleptolis, destroyer of cities; *Helandros*,
    destroyer of brave men.

CHORUS

> By such slight gestures does destiny
> approach. We think there is nothing strange
> or alarming, but it saunters up and then . . .
> a war!

FIRST CHORISTER

> She stepped from the silk of her canopied bed
> one ordinary morning, and by nightfall
> she was on that ship with its sails engorged by the winds,   560
> its oarsmen pulling hard, hard.
> In its wake a thousand ships would follow
> to Troy in pursuit, her moment's pleasure turned
> to their years of pain. For an evil woman, good
> soldiers spilled so much blood.

CHORUS

> A dour dower it was that she brought
> as her bride's portion: sacred vows were spoken
> at the marriage rite. And the pieties of the host
> and guest the Trojans knew and ought
> not to have broken.   570

FIRST CHORISTER

> A lesson in manners for Troy, one could call that war.
> The marriage hymn reverberated a long
> time, as the Trojan widows keened their grief
> in a different key in a song
> that curses the day Paris, kidnapper, thief,
> brought Helen ashore.

CHORUS

> It is said that a farmer reared
> a lion cub, a nursling that liked to play
> like any kitten, amusing the children, cute,
> nothing at all to be feared,   580
> until, one day,

full-grown, it reverted, became
that lion it always had been, and attacked the herd.
The yard, the house, were covered in blood and gore,
and grief also, and shame.
What he'd done was absurd.

FIRST CHORISTER
To the gods of ruin and death nobody prays;
to sacrifice to them would be redundant.

CHORUS
She was like that, an ornament,
the first trophy-wife, whose invitations   590
no one declined. It was love and fame and splendor,
but the gods' dire intent
was grief for that nation.

Their moments of joy were brief.
But joy is like that, engendering a litter
of tribulations. Those who are happy, we know
will come one day to grief.
Their tears will be bitter.

FIRST CHORISTER
That's true enough, but this was something else.
Iniquity's get is retribution and pain.   600
If virtue endures, its rewards also endure.

CHORUS
But assume that the virtuous man
prospers and then grows proud.
His pride, which is dangerous, can
cause him to fall. Hubris
operates often like this,
and the wailing is loud.

Righteousness dwells with the poor,
in a cottage, content, while the wealthy

men in their mansions need more,   610
no matter how much they've amassed.
Corrupt and spoiled, they at last
go mad. It's unhealthy.

FIRST CHORISTER

They forget the purpose of life, the hard truth
that there is a proper end to all things . . .
*(Agamemnon enters in a chariot with Cassandra. He is followed by a
portion of his retinue.)*

SECOND CHORISTER

Hail, great King! Destroyer of cities, Lord
Atreus' heir! How can we properly greet you?

FIRST CHORISTER

Not fulsomely, nor stintingly, but correctly,
in proper measure, in truth, as all things should be done.

SECOND CHORISTER

The feigning of greater emotion than anyone feels   620
is common enough. With true joy, as with deepest
sorrow, the words are the same, and the looks on men's faces.

FIRST CHORISTER

But the shepherd knows his flock and is not deceived.
The too-watered wine can never taste the same
as what comes fresh from the cask and into the ewer.

SECOND CHORISTER

We had our doubts, I confess, long years ago,
and spoke our minds as you readied your force for Troy.

FIRST CHORISTER

But that was then, and this is now. Our hearts
are full of love. We celebrate your success,

and rejoice in your homecoming. Time will make clear   630
how well your people have served you, how honest and loyal,
or else how not, as you resume your reign.

AGAMEMNON

Argos and its gods, I greet. It is right
and proper to do so, having maintained our right
at Troy, and having imposed on them the justice
they all deserved. Words are not unimportant,
but the gods, attending to deeds, cast their ballots
in the urn of blood and war. The other urn,
that of innocence, acquiescence, and peace,
no god came near except faint Hope. The smoke   640
still rises from those ruins and the reek
of burnt flesh even yet hangs in Troy's air.
For their gift of this success we thank the gods,
for revenge and the satisfaction of our honor.
For a woman we did these things, becoming midwives,
our apocalyptic mare having come into foal
in the dead of night with a brood of men-at-arms
ready to deal death as indifferent stars
wheeled away the hours high in the sky.
Their princes, huddled like sheep in a pen, were bleating   650
as our lions, having leaped their fence, attacked them
and lapped their fill of blood. For this, we thank
and praise the Olympian gods. Having said this,
we turn to your words, still fresh in our minds, and agree
there must be some sorting out. By nature, men
are contentious creatures, vying one with another.
Few there are who can truly rejoice in their neighbor's
good fortune. In most, envy and malice
taint the spirit. We fight to survive and thrive,
but along with the human condition's usual burdens   660
is covetousness that weighs heavy on the heart.
These years have taught me much. Professions of friendship
are easy to make, cost nothing, are less than a shadow's

shadow. Only in deeds is the truth revealed.
Of all my companions, only Odysseus, who sailed
against his will, proved faithful in every test
and never wavered. This I say of my friend,
not knowing whether he be now alive or dead.
    We shall appoint commissions. We will debate
together in conclave all these public questions   670
of religious and civil affairs, pronouncing approval
of what has been well done. To whatever is bad,
we will, as any good surgeon must, apply
the scalpel to debride the wounds and restore
to health and vigor the body of our state.
    I thank you all. I now complete my return,
crossing again the threshold of my palace
for which I have so long yearned. To my household gods
I offer greetings and thanks that I have been spared.
To Nike, the goddess Victory, I pray   680
that she may ever attend me, granting me still
her favor as she has done these many years.
(As he is about to descend from his chariot, Clytemnestra enters. She is
                    followed by attendants carrying tapestries they set
                            on the ground in front of the chariot.)

CLYTEMNESTRA
    Before you, men of Argos, our elders and statesmen,
I do not blush to confess my love for my husband.
We learn, as we grow older, to put aside
our maidenly diffidence. I prefer plain speaking.
    Simply and directly, then, I say
how these long years I have waited at home for my husband
besieging distant Troy. A sad and lonely
vigil it was, and full of fears, as I listened,   690
or rather tried not to listen, to each new rumor,
tried not to let my imagination run wild,
compounding disaster upon disaster. Killed?

Maimed? Wounded? If every report I heard
were true of my husband's having been hurt in battle,
he'd have been filled with as many holes as a net
the fisherman throws in the sea. They brought dispatches
over and over again announcing his death—
as if he had more lives than a cat, as if
with the lopping of each of Geryon's heads a new   700
cortege appeared for the solemn rites of interment.
Grief upon grief by day, and then, each night,
terrible dreams. My friends and the servants noticed
whenever I glanced at the roof-beams: they read my mind
aright, knowing I looked for a place to fasten
that rope from which I could hang myself, or sash
or scarf . . . More than half mad I was, for in madness
I could find a kind of relief. The rational world
was insupportable, dreadful. Therefore, Orestes,
our son, whom I love and from whom I could take
                some comfort,   710
I sent away—to Strophius in Phocis,
who acts as his protector. I feared a report
of your death in Troy might result in disturbance here,
an insurrection in which event he'd have been
the obvious target. This is the sad truth.
     For myself, my fountain of tears ran utterly dry
years ago. My eyes were red with weeping,
and sore from rubbing, as I peered out every night
to look for the beacon fires to light the sky.
Exhausted, I'd fall asleep, but then some gnat's   720
buzz would rouse me from terrible dreams, and I'd peer
again through the window, in grief and torment, at nothing.
     But my lord has come back home to me, our savior,
the watchdog of our flock, the great roof-beam
securing our palace, the mast of our ship of state,
or, say, that glimpse of land for which the sailors,
so long storm-tossed, have given up all hope.

The night is ended, the storm has abated, and here
is the dawn that breaks in the eastern sky. The parched
and weakened traveler sees at last that brook   730
from which he can drink sweet water . . . Such is the fervor
with which we welcome him home, or so I should say
in even greater detail, were I not reluctant
to dare the gods, who measure the joys of men
in dollops, begrudging us happiness in excess.

    I pray you, my dear lord, as you dismount,
do not set the foot that has trampled down proud Troy
on common earth, but allow us to set out
rich weavings that you deserve.

(to her attendants)

                       Do not delay,
but do as I have instructed. The tapestries now   740
unroll before him, bright with the royal purple
in sign of respect as the goddess of justice demands.
All these years I have waited and planned this welcome
in every detail, as I knew in my heart the gods
would require of me. This is just the beginning.

AGAMEMNON

A long war, and a speech almost as long!
But I thank you, though the praises you heap upon me
would be better from elsewhere. Women do run on
at the mouth sometimes, but I don't like any fawning.
I'm no barbarian chieftain. No one need grovel   750
and bow and scrape . . . or strew my path with rugs.
The gods we can honor so. I'm a mere mortal,
and not too proud to set foot on my native earth.
This tapestry business is too much, and I am not
easy about it. That happiness you talk of
is all very well, but I call no man's life happy
until it has come to its end, as I hope mine will
in my old age, in peace, tranquil and painless.

CLYTEMNESTRA
    My lord, you are being perverse. Would you ruin my plans?

AGAMEMNON
    What about my plans? Who consulted me?   760

CLYTEMNESTRA
    This is absurd! Have you made some vow to the gods?

AGAMEMNON
    It is, indeed, absurd. And the question is closed.

CLYTEMNESTRA
    Would Priam have been so modest, if he had won?

AGAMEMNON
    Probably not. But what's that to do with me?

CLYTEMNESTRA
    Do you, then, unlike him, fear men's complaints?

AGAMEMNON
    The opinion of mankind is a very great thing.

CLYTEMNESTRA
    The only sure defense against man's envy
    is not to be enviable.

AGAMEMNON
                And what's the defense
    against the tongues of women?

CLYTEMNESTRA
                Victorious one,
    can you not yield this victory to your wife?   770

AGAMEMNON

Is this a victory any wife would want?

CLYTEMNESTRA

My lord, consent to it. Indulge my whim.

AGAMEMNON

If it means so much to you, let someone come
to undo my sandals. If I'm to walk on purple,
I'll do so with bare feet—to avoid the gods'
attention and even retribution. A silly
practice, to make a conspicuous waste of wealth!
(One of Clytemnestra's servants helps the king with his sandals. He
continues to speak, referring to Cassandra, who is
standing beside him.)
But I have agreed. In turn, I ask of you
that you receive this stranger in our household
with kindness. The gods approve a gentle master.   780
She is our household servant, the fairest flower
of all the spoils of Troy, my army's gift.
She follows in my train.
                                    Against my better
judgment, I walk this purple path before me
to enter once again my palace halls.

CLYTEMNESTRA

The sea will not dry up. There are plenty of fish
swimming about—those purpura they catch
to make the dye. And there's money left to buy it.
At such a time, we are not constrained.
We can afford an extravagant gesture like this.   790
What would I not have given or sacrificed,
if the oracle had asked it, to see you safely
home this way? Your life has been spared to me.
Nothing else can matter! One may trim

the limbs of a tree, but so long as the root is alive,
the life is there, and the leaves will come again
in vigor to shade the house from the hot sun's rays
in the terrible days of summer. You have come home,
and now all will be well again!
(Agamemnon goes into the palace.)

                                        One waits
and tries not to lose faith. The bitter grape   800
ripens at last, by the grace of Zeus, to sweetness,
and we can make wine in the autumn to drink together
in the evening cool with the lord of the household home . . .
I have waited long for this. O mighty Zeus,
fulfilling our plans and making our dreams come true,
in joy and reverence I thank you for this day!
(Clytemnestra goes into the palace.)

FIRST CHORISTER

Why are we not happy? Why
do our chests constrict in apprehension?
What should we fear? The time has long gone by
since Agamemnon sailed from Aulis' shore.   810
Whatever the gods' intention
for harm, it would have happened surely before
now. We are awake, but still we seem
trapped in a dream.

SECOND CHORISTER

The king has returned home. This should
comfort us, but the Erinyes never
relent. We know those things that are not good
here in Mycenae, and how evil begets
evil, and so on, forever.
There is always some repayment of those old debts,   820
or corrections, say, of mistakes one may have made.
Now we are afraid.

FIRST CHORISTER

What is health? Where is that fine
line where illness begins? And what
are happiness and prosperity?
Do they come from getting what we want,
or something else, something we never looked for?
In any event, they never last long,
health and happiness. Something goes wrong.
The timbers of this ship await   830
that rock they will founder on, their fate,
no matter how well the sailors fend,
throwing their cargo overboard at the end.

SECOND CHORISTER

Misery, though, endures, and the dead
stay dead forever, although it is said
that Aesculapius had the skill to revive
those who had gone. But for this offense
Zeus struck him down with a lightning bolt from the sky.
When the omens are bad, the only thing
to which our desperate hopes may cling   840
is that one god may dispute with another
and frustrate the dire plans of his brother.
This long-odds chance always remains,
perhaps to distract us from our pains.
(Clytemnestra enters and addresses Cassandra, who is still standing in
Agamemnon's chariot.)

CLYTEMNESTRA

You, too, Cassandra. Inside! You're one of us now.
It's hard to get used to, being a slave, but it happens.
Even great Heracles was sold as a slave
and had to learn to do a master's bidding.
Don't be so proud. Get down from the car
and be glad you're not the chattel of some new-rich   850
princeling where they don't know how to treat their servants.

Lucky for you, we have our ways in this house,
and servants, if they behave, have decent lives.
Get down, I say. We're about to perform the rite
at the god's altar to welcome the master home.
(*Cassandra doesn't move or even seem to notice.*)

SECOND CHORISTER

She's speaking to you. You'd better do as you're told.
If you like, you can think that it's destiny you obey
and not just her. But whatever you think, get down.
(*Clytemnestra tries again, this time with gestures.*)

CLYTEMNESTRA

You hear me, girl? You understand plain Greek?
You! Get down from the cart! You go inside!   860

FIRST CHORISTER

Go with her, lady. What else can you possibly do?
You have no choice, but must do as she has bidden.
(*Cassandra ignores them.*)

CLYTEMNESTRA

I haven't got all day for this! The victims
stand ready now at the altar awaiting the knife
as we mark this joyous moment we never believed
we'd live to see. You should come in now, or you'll miss it!
Are you deaf, perhaps? Do you hear a word I'm saying?

SECOND CHORISTER

Either she can't hear or she can't understand. She needs
some help. She just stands there like a wild woman.

CLYTEMNESTRA

Deaf, or perhaps she's mad. Maybe her mind   870
has snapped, being taken away from home that way.

She'll adjust in time, I'm sure. But I can't stand here
wasting my breath and waiting for it to happen.
(*Clytemnestra exits.*)

FIRST CHORISTER

We're not angry. There's nothing to be afraid of.
You can't stay up in that cart forever, you know.
Come, take a step down. You have to do it.

CASSANDRA

Otototoi! Popoi da!
Apollo! Appalling Apollo!

SECOND CHORISTER

She calls on Apollo, but what is she saying? And why
lament to him? He's not the right god for that.   880

CASSANDRA

Otototoi! Popoi da!
Apollo! Appalling Apollo!

FIRST CHORISTER

She calls out again to the same wrong god, who seems
in any event not to be paying attention.

CASSANDRA

Apollo! Lord of streets and doorways and journeys,
you have destroyed me a second time now, O god.

SECOND CHORISTER

She is perhaps about to utter to us
prophecies. That gift from the gods can persist,
I do believe, even in one who's enslaved.

CASSANDRA

    Apollo, my persecutor, and lord of journeys,   890
    is this my destination? To what kind of house
    have you brought me after all?

FIRST CHORISTER

    This is the house of Agamemnon, the son
    of Atreus. I tell you the truth, my child.

CASSANDRA

    A house that heaven hates! An abattoir,
    a shambles, a charnel house, a butcher shop
    where the blood that pools on the floor is that of kin.

SECOND CHORISTER

    She has heard the old stories, no doubt.

FIRST CHORISTER

                       Or knows
    something. Or only suspects and guesses?

CASSANDRA

    I see it plainly, the babies wailing, their blood   900
    flowing, their flesh roasted and carved, and their father
    before my horrified eyes, eating, eating . . .

SECOND CHORISTER

    We have heard of her soothsaying gifts. But Mycenae is not
    in any great need these days of prophets and seers.

CASSANDRA

    It's a monstrous business that wicked Clytemnestra
    has planned for us all. Horror, horror on horror,
    beyond endurance or even imagination,

and anyone who could prevent it or intercede
is far away.

FIRST CHORISTER

I can't guess how she does this, but what she's saying   910
we all understand too well, for she speaks our fears.

CASSANDRA

Terrible woman! How can you do this thing?
This is your husband, the bedmate you have loved.
You go to him in his bath . . . He smiles to see you
approach. You stretch forth your hand to him . . . How can you
do what even I cannot bear to watch?

SECOND CHORISTER

I understood for a while, but now she's lost me.
What does she mean? What is she talking about?

CASSANDRA

Oh, no! A fisherman's net! The pity, the pity!
That snare, and she is herself the bait, and the dogs   920
are savage, savage, barking and baying. Stone them!
For such crimes, culprits are stoned to death.

FIRST CHORISTER

Whatever it is, it's clear that it isn't good.
The avenging Furies mutter such imprecations
before they strike, and the marrow chills in my bones
to hear such words. We are wounded, bleeding, weak,
and waiting in pain for a death we begin to welcome.

CASSANDRA

I see! I see! The bull that stands in the meadow
is gored by his mate. Her black horn seeks his vitals,
and he falls . . . In water! Reddening with his blood!   930

It made me laugh to see the calf walk a mile and a half
to take a bath . . .

SECOND CHORISTER

She's quite mad. But madwomen sometimes tell us
what the world's madness proposes. What she has seen
before is horrid enough to let her see
the horrors that now are to come. I fear her words.

CASSANDRA

I could have died at home. What a very long voyage
to arrive at the same dark gate that welcomes us all
to end our afflictions. But I shall not die alone!

FIRST CHORISTER

She is possessed. She mourns like the nightingale   940
that iterates its lament for Itys, and Procne,
and all the griefs and cruelties of the world.

CASSANDRA

The nightingale is just a bird. Its cries
sound mournful perhaps to us, but have nothing of grief
in their sweet sounds. And grief, I see, is coming.

SECOND CHORISTER

Is this a mere figure of speech, or do you see,
truly? And how did you come by this prophet's gift?
So that we may better judge how far to trust them,
tell us the source of these dire prognostications.

CASSANDRA

Oh, the woe of Paris' marriage, the woe   950
of Scamander, that river of tears, beside whose banks
I used to sit. Now all the rivers are tears,
bitter as Cocytus, darker than Acheron.

SECOND CHORISTER

That's clear enough for a child to understand it.
We are grieved to hear of your pain, from which such wisdom
arises as you are prompted now to share.

CASSANDRA

Pain? Oh, yes, my pain! My city destroyed.
I weep for all the cattle my father killed . . .
Those sacrifices were useless, useless. The altars
are all torn down, and the temple's walls, and the city's,   960
but the fire blazes bright still in my soul,
and my walls, too, will fall soon enough to rubble.

FIRST CHORISTER

Could it be that these catastrophes you have survived
have bruised your spirit so that you see only grief
wherever you go? I mean no disrespect . . .
We sympathize and would help you if we could.

CASSANDRA

I shall speak more clearly to make you understand.
What I foretell need not, like some blushing bride,
peep out from behind its veil. But bold and blunt
as the sunshine's dazzle at morning, I shall enlighten   970
even the blind, who must feel if they cannot see.
Blood! Do you understand that? Human blood,
and the stink of it that has fouled these silent stones!
There is a chorus here—not you, but the Furies,
raging at sin and eager for retribution,
chanting their hatred of evil and bewailing the years
they have had to wait for the cleansing. Blood will have blood,
for Thyestes' sins! For a brother's defiling his brother's
marriage bed! For murder! Unspeakable crimes . . .
Are these expressions of psychic trauma or real,   980
the shameful truths you all know and fear to whisper
aloud or even to think of alone, in silence?

On your oath, I ask you: Do I shoot wide of the mark,
or does my arrow quiver there in the bulls-eye?

FIRST CHORISTER
You have no need of an oath from any of us,
but know our hearts and the troubles we all keep there.
You come from far away! How do you know,
as if you had grown up here, our city's secrets?

CASSANDRA
I have the gift from the god Apollo, himself.

SECOND CHORISTER
Was the god attracted . . . ? Was it as in the stories?   990

CASSANDRA
Up until now, I spoke about this in shame.

FIRST CHORISTER
We learn to live without modesty's luxury.

CASSANDRA
He was after me, eager, ardent, breathing hard . . .

FIRST CHORISTER
And did you at last give him what he wanted?

CASSANDRA
I said I would, but then I broke my promise.

SECOND CHORISTER
After he'd given this gift? Is that how it was?

CASSANDRA
And I'd already told the Trojans what would happen.

SECOND CHORISTER
Apollo must have been angry. What did he do?

CASSANDRA
His curse on me is that nobody ever believes me.

FIRST CHORISTER
But we believe what you say. Or, anyway, I do.   1000

CASSANDRA
But don't you see? It doesn't make any difference!
You can believe me or not, but there's nothing to do,
no way for you to change what is already written.
The pain has let go its perch in time and flies,
casting its shadow forward and back, as in dreams.
Do you not see those children, sitting there still
on the threshold, baleful, bloody, the cuts of their own
meat in their outstretched hands, the delicate organs
a cannibal's mixed grill? Can you not hear
their piteous cries? For this there must be vengeance!   1010
A lion lolls on the couch in that house and yawns,
showing enormous teeth. I must warn my master!
As a slave, I have a master, that lord of the fleet,
who conquered Troy and comes home now in his pride . . .
For what he did, a punishment waits upon him,
a faithful retainer, or say a companion dog
that licks his hand and wags its tail but may spring
at his neck, Até, at him. Attaboy!
Its ears lie flat on its head . . . Or is it a snake?
A serpent or, say, an amphisbaena, with heads   1020
and venomous fangs at both its monstrous ends.
A female, but bold enough to attack a man,
like Scylla, that lives on the rocks and preys on sailors.
It's a bitch and it snarls and waits, pretending gladness
to see the master home, but thinking blood,
blood . . . And there's nothing to do, no way to stop it.
My words are motes in the empty air that a bird

swoops through, diving, screaming what is to come.
But you will blame me and soon complain to me
that what I have said is all too true and horrid.   1030

FIRST CHORISTER
    I understand well enough Thyestes' feast
    of his children's flesh and tremble to hear that tale
    once more and its shameful truth. The rest is murky.
    I do not follow. Lions? Serpents? Bitches?

CASSANDRA
    I say that you shall behold Agamemnon's corpse.

SECOND CHORISTER
    You're sure of this? Perhaps, if you hadn't said it . . .

CASSANDRA
    It makes no difference. There's no way out. No hope.

SECOND CHORISTER
    May the gods forbid . . .

CASSANDRA
                    It's the gods who are doing this.

FIRST CHORISTER
    But why? To punish whom and for what sin?

CASSANDRA
    You haven't understood a thing I've said.   1040

FIRST CHORISTER
    To begin with, who is the lion? Give us a hint . . .

CASSANDRA
    I am speaking in idiomatic Attic Greek.

FIRST CHORISTER
  They do at Delphi, too, but what do they mean?

CASSANDRA
  I can feel the burning. Oh, how it comes! Ototoi!
  Appalling Apollo! The lioness has two feet
  and sleeps, when her mate is away, with a starveling wolf.
  It's death. For everyone, death. And for me, too,
  I am spared being spared. The knives are sharp, and
                    their whetstone
  is hatred, an anger that's boiled and seethed for years.
(*She breaks her prophet's wand and throws it to the ground.*)
  Destruction I have prophesied; now I destroy   1050
  my prophetess' paraphernalia. I can avenge
  myself, at least, on this poor inanimate object.
  It has lost its grip. We can let go one another.
  The god can take back that gift he turned to a curse.
  I am done with insults and mockers' disbelief.
  With friends and even kinfolk turned against me,
  the princess I'd been was turned to a sideshow gypsy,
  a diversion, an embarrassment, a joke . . .
  I bore it all, but now the show is closing.
  Instead of offering prayers at my father's altars   1060
  at home, I go myself as the sacrifice.
  I can feel already the heat of the knife blade
  that will butcher me like a beast. But heaven will note
  my death in its ledgers, and I shall be avenged
  with royal blood for my own royal blood. There comes
  from exile far away a child of this house
  to slay his father's murderer, his mother.
  The bloody walls of this palace of evil need
  that baneful capstone he will supply, but the gods,
  who see all things, have sworn an oath on the corpse   1070
  of the fallen king that the son will come to do
  and do and do. As is only right and proper.
  I make no complaint. I watched the fall of Troy.

Over the tongues of fire hot air shimmered,
and I could read there the sentences heaven had passed
on each of our captors and take from these some comfort.
I am comforted yet and am unafraid to face
those dismal gates through which I now must venture
where Death has been waiting to greet me. I pray that my killer's
stroke be swift and sure, and my passage easy   1080
into the dark where the horrors perhaps will end
and my eyes that have seen so much can close at last.

FIRST CHORISTER
    Oh, sad woman. Your speech is wise, indeed,
    and difficult for us to bear to hear.
    How can you look on your own death with such calm,
    such equanimity? You are like those oxen
    that, decked with garlands, amble on their own
    to the waiting altars of their sacrifice.

CASSANDRA
    They have no choice. There's nowhere else to go,
    no place to turn, for them or for me, either.   1090

SECOND CHORISTER
    You just stand still. You can wait or linger a little?

CASSANDRA
    Nothing would change. Would you have me flee? Where to?

FIRST CHORISTER
    I must say that we all admire your courage.

CASSANDRA
    That's a compliment nobody likes to hear.

SECOND CHORISTER
    If we all must die, a noble death is best.

CASSANDRA
I wish my father had had one, and his children.
(*She recoils in horror.*)

FIRST CHORISTER
Lady, what is it? What startles you?

CASSANDRA
                              Oh, gods!
Horrible, horrible!

FIRST CHORISTER
            What is the horror? What?
Does it start to sink in now? Does your nerve fail you?

CASSANDRA
No, it's disgust. The whole house stinks of blood.   1100

SECOND CHORISTER
It's the sacrifice they're making. These things are gory.

CASSANDRA
It reeks of corruption. It makes a person gag.

FIRST CHORISTER
I'll grant you, it isn't exactly *eau de lilas.*

CASSANDRA
I've had enough. I leave you to go inside
to groan for Agamemnon and for myself.
It's not so bad—a coming home to roost.
Remember this. For my blood, blood will spill,
another woman's blood. And for her husband's,
another man will die. It will come to pass
just as I've told you it would. Then, think of me   1110
and this day of my death. You won't be able to help it.

CHORUS

    Poor woman! As you take these fatal steps,
    we pity you.

CASSANDRA

           One last word, gentlemen.
    I offer a prayer to Apollo, in whose bright light
    I stand for the last time. Bear witness now.
    They are killing a slave, which is easy and therefore shameful.
    Punish them for this and make them suffer.
    Riches and power are nothing: a shadow's breath
    can make them disappear. Harder to bear
    is that misery, too, is nothing, a child's rude scrawl   1120
    on a writing slate that a damp sponge wipes away.
(She leaves the stage and enters the palace.)

FIRST CHORISTER

    This is perhaps the reason that rich men are greedy,
    knowing how wealth is temporary. This house,
    however large it may loom, is a moment's dream
    from which we may all at any moment wake.
    To King Agamemnon, the gods gave Troy and honor
    and a safe trip home . . . to this? To retribution?
    To die, himself, for the deaths he and his house
    have owed on eternity's ledger? So much for greatness!
(From the palace, a shriek is heard.)

AGAMEMNON *(offstage)*

    I am hit! Oh! Oh! Deep in the gut!   1130

SECOND CHORISTER

    Did you hear that? Did someone cry out?

AGAMEMNON *(offstage)*

                    Again!
    I am hit again! Oh!

FIRST CHORISTER
                    I think that's it.
      It's happened. What shall we do?

SECOND CHORISTER
                              What *can* we do?

FIRST CHORISTER
      Sound an alarm?

SECOND CHORISTER
                    What for? What would *they* do,
      whoever they are, who might come?

FIRST CHORISTER
                              We have to do something!

SECOND CHORISTER
      Why? If there's nothing to do?

FIRST CHORISTER
                              It's bloody murder!

SECOND CHORISTER
      You think? But how do you know that?

FIRST CHORISTER
                              Regicide!
      It's a coup d'état! The overthrow of the state!

SECOND CHORISTER
      It certainly sounds that way, but how can we know?

FIRST CHORISTER
      We could go and see?

SECOND CHORISTER
We can't. We're only the chorus.   1140
We can never leave this space. It's one of the rules.

FIRST CHORISTER
Are you out of your mind?

SECOND CHORISTER
I only wish I were.
This is too dreadful. How are we to endure it?

FIRST CHORISTER
If we're only the chorus, I'm sure we'll find a way.
Meanwhile, we have to find out what has happened.
Would someone
open the inner curtain so we can see?
(The inner curtain opens to reveal, in the interior of the palace, the
bodies of Agamemnon and Cassandra.
Clytemnestra is standing over them, still holding a
bloody dagger.)

CLYTEMNESTRA
All right, I lied. I had to, didn't I?
I'm not ashamed of that! What else could I do?
How else could I get the man I hated to trust me,
or at least to let down his guard for the moment I needed?   1150
I had all these years in which to plan it out,
going over it in my mind—I admit
with no small pleasure—and this was the best way.
That old score is settled at last. I killed him,
struck him down. I don't deny it! I'm proud
of what I've done! I threw his robe around him,
a net on a haul of fish, and he couldn't see,
or fight, or escape, and I stabbed him. Twice!
And each time, he groaned and then went quiet and limp,
and I stabbed him again. Three times, lucky! And prayed   1160

to Zeus, the lord of the living and also the dead,
for allowing me this wonderful fulfillment.
He bled like a pig! It spurted out and splashed me,
and I was delighted. A farmer, wet in the rain
of the spring that will give him his crops, could not be more
happy and grateful than I was then! I bloomed
like a whole garden of flowers in that downpour
of Agamemnon's blood.
                      You're not saying much.
Congratulate me, why don't you? Wish me well,
and rejoice with me. You can't say he didn't deserve it!   1170
It was right and proper—the least I could have done.
I'll pour a bitter libation over his corpse,
a cocktail of vintage evils he'd mixed for himself.
And now his royal cup is drained. All gone!

FIRST CHORISTER

I don't know how to reply to such a speech.
It's certainly clear, even blunt. But what can one say?

CLYTEMNESTRA

What difference does it make to me? Or to him?
There he is, on the floor. You can praise, or blame,
or accuse me of not behaving like a lady—
but you're not going to bring him back. With this right hand   1180
I did the job right, and it can't be undone.

SECOND CHORISTER

Woman, this is not good! Are you on drugs?
This is crazy! To do such a thing is mad . . .
But then to announce it this way? To stand there, shameless,
red-handed, as they say? You've killed the king!
You've murdered your husband! What are we in the city
to make of this? And what can happen now?
People will hate you! Fear you! What is your plan
now? Are you going off somewhere into exile?

CLYTEMNESTRA

Whatever for? You threaten *me* with exile?   1190
You talk to me, now, of the people's hatred?
What about then? What about him? What hatred
did any of you have for a man like that
who killed his own daughter? A sacrifice!
He couldn't find a sheep? So he kills his child?
My child! From out of my body! He couldn't wait
for the goddamned winds to shift for his ships to sail on?
What kind of evil is that, or madness? He,
he is the one you should have hated and banished.
But not a word from you. Not a look. Nothing!   1200
And you criticize me? Upon what ground?
As long as the army takes orders from me, you watch it.
You keep your insolent mouths shut, you hear?
Or I will shut them for you, forever. You hear me?

FIRST CHORISTER

This is no way to talk! Has your bloody deed
unsettled your mind, perhaps? Is this stress-related?
I assure you, we're trying our best to understand.

CLYTEMNESTRA

If I am possessed, I say it is by the gods.
Diké, the god of Justice, avenging Até . . .
These are the spirits to whom I have sacrificed   1210
this man at my feet. I was not afraid and am not
afraid now. Aegisthus is still loyal,
and if he and I are together, whom should we fear?
I have not lost my reason. You know my reasons!
Iphigenia! And then, at Troy, Chryseïs,
and later this one, Cassandra—and who knows how many
others have shared his bed? They deserved to die.
She sang her little swan-song and I killed her,
and rather enjoyed it, too. An extra treat!

FIRST CHORISTER

Our king is laid low. For a woman he fought;   1220
by a woman's hand he died.
How shall we bear his pain? How ought
we to behave toward his killer
who once was his bride?

SECOND CHORISTER

Helen, who brought death to many men,
gets the credit for yet one more.
Blood bespatters her royal raiment again
that will never wash away
from him, dead on the floor.

CLYTEMNESTRA

I tell you again to watch what you say, mister.   1230
You can't blame Helen for all these deaths. My sister
and I were victims. The two of us suffered, too.
Repeat those words you just said
and you're likely to wind up dead.

FIRST CHORISTER

Tantalus' heirs, Agamemnon and Menelaus,
inherited this curse of blood that cried
for blood. The price they pay is
dear indeed, as the woman he married stands
with the bloody knife in her hands,
crowing aloud in her pride.   1240

SECOND CHORISTER

Helen, who brought death to many men,
gets the credit for yet one more.
Blood bespatters her royal raiment again
that will never wash away
from him, dead on the floor.

CLYTEMNESTRA
> It's surely the truth that this house carries a curse:
> Infanticide, cannibalism, and worse
> are the sons' of Atreus heritage of horror.
> For what had been done, the gods willed
> that more blood would have to be spilled.   1250

FIRST CHORISTER
> It is always a terrible fate
> when the wrath of the gods is great.
> Oh, woe, woe upon woe,
> that it must be ever so.
> What can mere mortals do
> but what the gods order us to?

SECOND CHORISTER
> Alas for the dead king.
> How shall I speak or sing
> our grief while his voice is stilled?
> By the hand of his wife, he was killed,   1260
> as a spider will murder a fly
> that is caught in its web. And we cry,
> "Oh, woe upon woe."

CLYTEMNESTRA
> You think it was me? It only looks that way.
> Think of me as the ghost of Atreus. Say
> he did it, using my hand, that man who would serve
> his brother his own children's meat. They deserve
> whatever they get, this child-slaughtering clan.
> I was the agent, perhaps, but his was the plan.

FIRST CHORISTER
> Are you claiming that you had nothing to do with it, then,   1270
> and that you were merely the tool of more powerful men?

Call it Chaos, Ares' bloodlust, whatever
you will . . . But you are stained with this deed forever.

SECOND CHORISTER
Alas for the dead king.
How shall I speak or sing
our grief while his voice is stilled?
By the hand of his wife, he was killed,
as a spider will murder a fly
that is caught in its web. And we cry,
"Oh, woe upon woe."   1280

CLYTEMNESTRA
He was innocent then, a blameless father
and faithful husband, come home to the wicked mother?
The judges of Hell will know how to deal with the ghost
of a man like this. My Iphigenia is lost,
and he did that. He did it—to her and to me!
The consequence of that is what you see.

FIRST CHORISTER
I am afraid. Where can we hide? Where
can we look for shelter? Blood falls thick in the air
like the rain of a summer shower.
Now, in this bitter hour,   1290
we are frightened and stricken dumb,
as we wait for more evil to come.

SECOND CHORISTER
I wish I were dead and my body were laid in the earth.
This day is the worst since the day of my birth.
Who shall bury the king? Who shall mourn
his death in the proper way? My heart is torn!
If you perform those funeral rites, you will

blaspheme the gods, and add much to the ill
you've already accomplished. At the bier
of this fallen hero, who will shed a tear?   1300

CLYTEMNESTRA

Your silver heads needn't worry on that account.
I, who killed him, will lower him into his grave.
Let Iphigenia below greet him with kisses
or however she will on the lovely occasion that this is.

FIRST CHORISTER

You are a hard woman, but still, it is plain,
that, sooner or later, the slayer in turn is slain.
Zeus, on his throne, keeps order and balance below.
Can the violence ever end? Or will it go
on and on, as bad gives way now to worse
calamity in this sad house, on which there's a curse?   1310

SECOND CHORISTER

I wish I were dead and my body were laid in the earth.
This day is the worst since the day of my birth.
Who shall bury the king? Who shall mourn
his death in the proper way? My heart is torn!
If you perform those funeral rites, you will
blaspheme the gods, and add much to the ill
you've already accomplished. At the bier
of this fallen hero, who will shed a tear?

CLYTEMNESTRA

I'll look to the gods on my own, and take my chances.
My spirit, after all these years of torment,   1320
is at rest at last. That demon is done
with our house and now can go wherever he's sent.
I only wish I could go, too. I have hated this
place since the day I came. What a horror it is!
(Aegisthus enters, accompanied by armed guards.)

AEGISTHUS
>The day of retribution has come, and the gods
>can look down in its light on crimes avenged.
>I look at this corpse in a robe the Erinyes wove,
>who demand that men make payments and settle accounts.
>His father Atreus drove forth from this city
>Thyestes, who was his brother and my father.   1330
>You all know the appalling story. My father
>came home, a suppliant, asking his brother's protection.
>And Atreus, Agamemnon's father, promised
>not merely life and safety but a warm welcome,
>a celebration, a feast—and at that banquet
>he served up for my father my brothers' flesh.
>He broke their little fingers and toes and arrayed
>these pieces on the platter of broiled meat—
>human meat! Long pig . . . But what did my father
>know? Who could suspect or even imagine   1340
>so beastly a thing? The poor man ate that dinner
>whereupon Atreus told him what it was.
>My father cried out, vomited forth his children,
>and cursed the depraved house of Pelops forever.
>I am glad this man is dead. I have lived to see it,
>have schemed and plotted and bided my time. His father
>drove my father away, with me, the remaining
>infant son, helpless, in swaddling clothes.
>But little babies grow at last to manhood,
>and from exile one can return, from the ends of the earth,   1350
>as I have, to see this lovely thing accomplished.

>I can die happy now, for no one can take
>the sweetness of this moment I'll keep forever
>in a heart that my early suffering so hardened.

FIRST CHORISTER
>Aegisthus, it is unseemly to gloat over corpses.
>This murder is no cause for rejoicing or pride.

Quite the reverse, in fact, and you shall face
the people's righteous anger. Death by stoning?
Something like that, I believe, is what the statute
prescribes for such an offense.

AEGISTHUS

                        You're threatening me?   1360
Amusing, if I may say so. You hold an oar,
down in the galley, chained as you are to the benches,
but I'm up here on deck where we steer the vessel.
We decide where to go. You just do as you're told
and pray not to be whipped. Old as you are,
there are lessons you need to study—in tact and prudence.
My pedagogy is harsh but not ineffective,
as you'll see when your masters, hunger and pain, appear
to drill you in proper manners. The learning curve
is very steep, I assure you.

SECOND CHORISTER

                        Your talk is brave,   1370
but during the recent war, you, like a woman,
waited here at home for the men to come back.
You lolled in a hero's bed, and on his pillows
planned his disgraceful death. How brave was that?

AEGISTHUS

Brave or not, it wasn't reckless and stupid
as you are being now. You'll eat those words.
With his voice, Orpheus charmed the birds in the trees;
your deplorable croaking will summon vipers.
You shall soon feel my anger's venom, I promise.

FIRST CHORISTER

As if *you* could be the master here in Argos!   1380
You've gone quite mad! You plotted this death, perhaps,

but you didn't have nerve enough to wield the knife.
To strike the blow yourself? Oh, dear me, no!

AEGISTHUS

It wouldn't have made any sense. The woman tricked him
as I could never have done. He knew who I am,
and knew my reasons for hating him as I did.
I'd never have had the easy chance that she did.
But I have the treasury now and, with it, the army
that will do as I command, as you'll soon see.

SECOND CHORISTER

Another demonstration, if I may say so,   1390
of shamelessness and the want of personal valor!
Our city's gods have not abandoned us. They
will overthrow you soon enough. Orestes
is still alive somewhere, and with their help
may one day come back home for blood and vengeance.

AEGISTHUS

Sedition! Treason!
(to his men-at-arms)
                                  Arrest them, every one.

FIRST CHORISTER

I warn you, we have swords, too.

SECOND CHORISTER

                                  And we're the chorus!
You can't arrest us. It isn't allowed.

AEGISTHUS

                                  We'll see.
Who forbids it? They'll have to answer to me.

FIRST CHORISTER

I'm happy for fortune and courage and skill to decide   1400
the issue between us. In none of those, I think,
do you seem richly endowed.

SECOND CHORISTER

Come on, let's fight!

CLYTEMNESTRA *(interfering at last)*

No, my darling, not now. There's been enough
bloodshed for one day.
(to the Chorus)
You, sirs, go home.
We have done what we have had to do. For you,
we've no ill will. We wish none of you harm.
Therefore, to each of your houses, go at once.
This is your queen's advice. Be wise, and take it.

AEGISTHUS

They should learn to tame their tongues. These doddering men
insulted me! They ought to be taught good manners.   1410

FIRST CHORISTER

From you, barbarian? Brute? Coward? We do not
cringe at the like—or even dislike—of you!

AEGISTHUS

You have not yet heard the last of this.

SECOND CHORISTER

Or you,
if fate bring Orestes home.

AEGISTHUS

                    Fat chance of that!
I've been an exile. I know what it's like out there,
living on hope.

FIRST CHORISTER

                    It's better than living on shit, and getting fat
as you've been doing here.

AEGISTHUS

                    You watch your mouth!

SECOND CHORISTER

You're like a rooster, crowing on a dunghill.

FIRST CHORISTER

Or mounted up on his hen.

CLYTEMNESTRA

                    Who cares what they say?
You and I are the masters here, remember?   1420
(*Blackout*)

The Libation Bearers

Cast

ORESTES, son of Agamemnon and Clytemnestra
PYLADES, Orestes' friend
ELECTRA, Orestes' sister
CHORUS of foreign serving-women
CLYTEMNESTRA, now wife of Aegisthus, queen of Argos
CILISSA, Orestes' nurse
AEGISTHUS, king of Argos
SERVANT of Clytemnestra and Aegisthus
NONSPEAKING
    Attendants of Orestes, Clytemnestra, and Aegisthus

(The tomb of Agamemnon in Argos. Orestes and Pylades enter.)

ORESTES
    Hermes, our medium, herald of great Zeus,
    hear me! And save me, I beg you. I have returned
    from exile and, here at home at my father's grave-mound,
    kneel in prayer and offer a lock of my hair
    to Inachus, the river god of Argos,
    as a pledge of faith—the offering I should have made
    with my hand on the lid of the coffin that terrible day
    they laid the king in the ground.
                    But what is this?
    Who are these people, this gaggle of women who come
    to the graveyard, black as a murder of crows? Has new   10
    catastrophe come upon Argos, some fresh sorrow
    to afflict this house? Or do they yet mourn my father
    and offer these libations on his account
    to the gods below.
                I hope it's that.
                      Electra!
    It's her, my sister, leading the mourning women.

Oh Zeus, be gracious. Give me strength. Let me
avenge my father's murder.
                    Pylades,
let us conceal ourselves. I want to listen
to what they're saying and find out what's going on.
(Orestes and Pylades exit. Then, after a moment, Electra enters, leading a
chorus of women carrying libations.)

FIRST CHORISTER

We come in this sorry train,   20
raking our cheeks bloody,
preferring this to the pain
of the soul. The hurt of the body
is easy enough to bear
compared to this nightmare
from which we seem somehow unable to wake.
For the dead king, for Agamemnon's sake,
we come here, or for his shade
that haunts Clytemnestra and makes her so afraid.
We hear her cries of anguish every night.   30
Mother Earth, we pray you, make it right.

SECOND CHORISTER

How can this bloodguilt be
cleansed? The house is in mourning,
but this enrages her. She
hears in a groan a warning.
We are forced in our grief to grin
as we try to ignore that sin
that taints the very air of this house of woe.
But she is the queen, and insists we behave as though
there were no righteousness, no laws   40
to restrain the ambitions of men or give them pause
with retribution or punishment, but the will
of the gods is just, and they are powerful still.

FIRST CHORISTER

    The respect we had for majesty is gone.
    What is there now to revere or admire? Fear
    is sovereign now in the hearts of men. That yoke
    is heavy and chafes our necks.
    But the scales of Justice will balance at last as the sun
    cuts through the darkness and burns the corruption away.
    In our grief, we wait for that day.   50

SECOND CHORISTER

    The earth of Argos, saturated with gore,
    is turning to red mud. Likewise, the souls
    of the guilty cannot withstand any further pang,
    but in utter misery thrill
    with remorse for what the rest of us deplore.
    At night in bed, their torments are at their worst.
    Relentlessly, they are cursed.

FIRST CHORISTER

    But what can we do? Like slaves, we must submit.
    Freedom is merely illusion, a dreamlike thing,
    for Fate is the master of all of us, though it   60
    seems cruel and hard to bear, indeed. In secret,
    we mourn for our dead king.

ELECTRA

    You women, my attendants, my friends, what can I say?
    Advise me how to perform this uncomfortable rite
    without untruth, without offense.
    How can I frame my prayer as I pour out the wine
    on my father's grave? That it comes from our house with love?
    From his loving wife, for instance? I cannot presume
    to speak on behalf of my mother or anyone else.
    All I can ask is that he intercede for us all   70
    and pray the gods to return goodness for goodness,
    and evil and pain to match evil and pain.

To utter such a prayer is blasphemous, shameful.
But to pour out the wine in utter and abject silence . . . ?
What kind of daughter could do that? Can I just turn away
as if I had made my libation over a midden
of kitchen refuse? Advise me! In love or pity,
tell me what I should say. Freewoman and slave,
we are sisters in pain. Tell me, what shall I do?

FIRST CHORISTER

In reverence for your late father, and also for you,   80
and in love and pity, too, we speak our minds.

ELECTRA

By my father's grave, I charge you. Tell me the truth.

FIRST CHORISTER

First of all, pray. As you pour the wine, invoke
the favor of all the gods on those who are loyal.

ELECTRA

And who are they? How can the gods tell?

FIRST CHORISTER

Yourself, of course. And any who hate Aegisthus.

ELECTRA

And that, I assume, would include you women here?

FIRST CHORISTER

That is for you to decide. Believe in no one,
but watch how they behave and note what they do.

ELECTRA

We, then, who are here at the grave, but who else is there?   90

FIRST CHORISTER
Remember your brother Orestes is far away
but alive. You can believe in him and hope.

ELECTRA
Yes, you have spoken well. Somewhere is Orestes.

SECOND CHORISTER
But do not forget those who have blood on their hands.

ELECTRA
I can never forget them. But what should I pray for them?

SECOND CHORISTER
That someone, some god or mortal, may come one day . . .

ELECTRA
As judge, you mean? As avenger?

SECOND CHORISTER
                                    Say it plainly,
as executioner, as one who will take a life
for the life they have taken.

ELECTRA
                          And can one pray for that?
Is it decent or right to ask such a thing of heaven?   100

SECOND CHORISTER
You are asking merely that heaven enforce its own laws.

ELECTRA
Hermes, our medium, herald of great Zeus
and nuncio to the world of the shades, hear me

and summon for me those ghosts from the underworld
to whom I pray, the spirits who guard my father's
ruined house. To you and to Earth herself,
who nurtures us all and receives us again to her bosom,
I offer my prayers with the purification of wine
I spill on the ground and offer here to the dead,
my father's ghost among them. I ask your compassion.   110
Have mercy on me and my dear brother Orestes,
wherever he is. How shall we be lords here,
princess and prince, and take our rightful places,
who now are powerless, outcast, or exiled,
despised by our city and even our own mother
who bore us and nursed us once as babes? She has swapped
both her children for Uncle Aegisthus, her sorry
bedmate and partner in crime in your own murder.
I am a servant here, a slave, and my brother
roams the earth, a vagrant, alone and impoverished.   120
They loll meanwhile in those luxuries you won
on the battlefield, taking that ease they earned
with their single treacherous deed. But Orestes may come,
may reappear any time . . . And this is my prayer.
Grant it, father. Bring him home, soon, soon.
And keep me true and chaste—I am not like my mother!
     But beyond these prayers on our own behalf,
I ask you to do what is right for your own sake:
avenge your murder. Let someone appear to maintain
justice and slay those two who have unjustly   130
slain! (Can I pray for evil? But how can I not,
at such a time and place? O gods, forgive me!)
Bless us here in the world above, and show us
your favor and grace, who, sorely afflicted, need it.
(*She pours the libation.*)
     I have done my part. I pour the libation.
It is now up to you to join me in lamentation,
braiding your prayers with mine in a woeful garland
as we chant to the dead we love and mourn together.

CHORUS

> Our tears pour forth and splash on the ground like rain
> for our fallen king. We come to this hallowed place   140
> to remember him and beg his protection.
> Hear us, O Agamemnon. We cry in pain
> for ourselves and for your children in their disgrace.
> Rouse yourself and rise in your shroud, and bring
> some sudden and drastic correction.
> Save us, O warrior king,
> we beg you, who suffer here.
> Come, with your mighty spear.

(As they conclude, Electra discovers the lock of hair Orestes left at
the tomb.)

ELECTRA

> My father has heard our prayers, and has received
> the wine offering. But someone has been here . . .   150

FIRST CHORISTER

> What makes you say that? What have you found?

SECOND CHORISTER

>   Tell us!

ELECTRA

> A lock of hair someone has left here.

FIRST CHORISTER

>   Whose?
> A man's or a woman's?

ELECTRA

>   How would one know?

SECOND CHORISTER

> Old then, or young? Is it white? Or pepper-and-salt?

ELECTRA
The color is just like my own. It matches . . . exactly!

FIRST CHORISTER
Is someone mocking you then, do you suppose?

ELECTRA
What on earth for? Unless . . .

SECOND CHORISTER
                    What are you thinking?

ELECTRA
Who would come here to do this? With hair that matches
my own so exactly in color and texture?

FIRST CHORISTER
                         Orestes?

ELECTRA
It could be his. But do I dare even hope?   160

SECOND CHORISTER
Might he have come in disguise, in secret?

ELECTRA
                              He might,
or perhaps he only sent this, and someone else
placed it here at the grave . . .

FIRST CHORISTER
                         The pains of exile
are never dulled. We grieve that he is not here.

ELECTRA
A lock of hair, but enough to overthrow me
altogether. It's sharp as a sword and strikes

as deep as did the weapon that killed my father.
Some sympathetic townsman, perhaps? Some stranger
who having heard the story is moved to pity?
All I know for certain, is who it is not—   170
his wife, his killer, my mother who is no mother
but a madwoman now, a monster. Or is it my brother?
I cannot help but hope, and yet in fear
of disappointment and grief, I cannot hope.
It's torment: every moment, every breath,
protracts the exquisite pain that is my life.
        A messenger then? But wouldn't there be a message,
some kindly word for the sister who stayed at home,
some news? Can it be my spiteful mother's trick?
I'd throw it away . . . But how can I know what to do?   180
At my father's grave, I should be braver than this,
and resolute as a good daughter should be.
I fail. We often do, and pray that heaven
may understand and forgive us, imperfect mortals.
Are the dead perhaps indulgent, too? Oh, father!
It's hard, hard, this life . . .
(She kneels down and stares at the ground.)
                                But what is this?
Here, in the soft earth, footprints . . . Of two different people!
Whoever they were, they were here not long ago.
Two companions . . .
                        But what kind of woodsman could tell
just from looking at footprints who could have made them?   190
And yet, I know! It has to be!
(Orestes enters.)

ORESTES
                                It's me!
The first of your prayers is answered. I have come home.
The rest, we still have to pray for and work to achieve.

ELECTRA
        What are you saying? What prayers are you talking about?

ORESTES

    I heard it all. You prayed that I might return,
    and here I am.

ELECTRA

              I see. And am happy. But still,
    I fear it may be some trick. Are you an impostor?

ORESTES

    No, I assure you. If there's a plot, it isn't mine.
    If there is danger, I am the one at risk.

ELECTRA

    You're making jokes, as you've always done.

ORESTES

                     My sister,   200
    we must either cry or laugh. I had hidden myself
    and I saw and heard as you came to our father's grave
    to address your prayer. I watched as you found that lock
    of hair I had left. Hysterical tears or jokes
    are the only possible choices. I am your brother!
    You know my face, my voice . . . You know this woven
    sash you made on your loom with your own hands.

ELECTRA

    Oh, most beloved, my dear brother! My father's
    child and the only hope of this house for the future,
    you have come home, and are three times welcome here: 210
    I love you as my father's son; that love
    a girl should feel for her mother I transfer
    to vest in you; and then, with a sibling's love
    that I had for Iphigenia I endow you,
    the only one left alive to whom I'm a sister.
    May Zeus, who takes delight in mystic triads,
    grant you his favor and give you the strength you shall need
    to accomplish that dangerous work you have before you.

ORESTES

    Zeus! Zeus! Look down on the orphaned brood
    of a mighty eagle. That noble bird is slain,   220
    caught in the dreadful coils of a venomous snake.
    How are those poor chicks still in the nest
    to survive? They are famished, and, not yet grown, how can they
    hunt and bring their father's quarry home?
    So you may look down at us, Electra
    and me, the bereft children, poor outcasts,
    the nestlings, as it were, of that mighty man
    who sacrificed to you and whose high purpose
    was nothing less than the work of the gods on earth.
    A serious life he led, and if his children   230
    are left to languish, to be destroyed, what heroes
    will look to you and pay you homage? Destroy
    us and you break faith with all mankind!
    Men believe that kings rule by the grace
    and favor of gods. Where is that grace or favor
    now? What hand will serve you at what altars?
    If you withdraw from the business of mankind,
    men will diminish, but gods will do so, too,
    to become abstractions, mere ideas of themselves.
    Help us! Raise us up! Restore yourself   240
    by restoring justice and us to our royal power.

CHORUS

    Not so loud. Someone will overhear.
    The walls have ears. There are spies everywhere. Men talk,
    and our masters listen—whose corpses I pray to see
    roasting in their pyres' pitchy smoke.

ORESTES

    It doesn't matter. Either I am protected,
    Apollo's particular creature and instrument
    of the gods' justice, or else there are no gods
    and there is no justice—in which case life is worthless.
    How do we value a human life, or a prince   250

or even a king? Can they work out compensation
of so-and-so many gold coins? The debt is of blood
and its satisfaction must be in blood—either theirs
or my own. As everyone in Argos knows.
There are wrongs in the world, and the powers of darkness
                    are loosed
to infect the earth and foul the air with plagues.
The healthy flesh, corrupted, will ulcerate,
and leprous lesions blossom everywhere
among the fungal encrustations eating
the suffering bodies away. Thus did the sun-god   260
explain what the Erinyes propose, stirred up as they are
by the evil here of victims unavenged.
Reason, order, and health are frail, and madness
threatens from every side. They are quite mad,
but I am, too. My dreams are of blood and torment,
and out of the darkness monsters on every side
menace and taunt. They are not to be endured.
I am a man accursed. I have roamed the earth
an exile no one welcomes, unclean . . . I cannot
approach an altar anywhere or touch   270
a festive wine-bowl with this taint I bear.
What prudent man would have me at his table
or let me pass a night beneath his roof?
I am, myself, a dead man or, say, a ghost
that cannot rest. I come to complain and haunt
those who have done me evil. What can I fear?
I put my trust in the gods, or else in the godless
void in which we can do whatever we want,
whatever we can imagine—and I can imagine
nothing else! What life I have is this   280
single deed, to which I believe the gods
prompt me and urge me on, and my father's spirit
commands, and my own grief, unassuaged, dictates.
    This is a great people. We conquered Troy.
These gallant men are proud and will not suffer
the rule of a pair of women—for he is a woman

as surely as she, and as likely to be pierced
in warm wet places by the sharp sword I wield.

CHORUS

O fates, your power that comes from Zeus is great.
Yours is the rule we live by, that evil demands   290
evil in turn. And here Orestes stands
ready to claim his due. How long must he wait?

ORESTES

Oh, my father, far away in the dark,
what comfort can I bring you? I believe
it is not enough that your children love you and grieve.
There must be a hope of justice, some faint spark.

FIRST CHORISTER

Young man, take comfort. The dead know very well
how to be patient. Now, let us chant that dirge
that resonates in our hearts, which in turn will urge
our action. The guilty will suffer. Time will tell.   300

ELECTRA

Hear us, O father, exiles, orphans, we come
to your tomb: it is now the only home we have.
Here we are, brother and sister, creatures of doom,
hurt and enraged but together at your grave.

SECOND CHORISTER

The wind in the trees is keening, but the key
may change as the weather shifts. It always does.
The tune may modulate to an ode that we
may sing in the palace together with good cause.

ORESTES

He should have died at Troy, in battle with honor.
We could have mourned our loss but taken pride   310

in his noble deeds. But murdered in this manner?
He is disgraced! And we are horrified.

FIRST CHORISTER

In the underworld, though, as a king they welcomed him.
It must have been thus in Hades' throne room. All
his comrades are there, the heroes and chiefs from the war,
gather around him in whatever faint and dim
version they have of rejoicing there, and they call
his name and praise him. Surely that matters more
than those brief moments inside
and the way in which he died.   320

ELECTRA

To talk thus of Troy and the war is to miss
the point. To pick among other possible stories
is a child's game. Our father was murdered, killed,
and the killers must pay. Let us think only of this
and not distract ourselves with irrelevant glories
of distant battles. Instead, let the world be filled
with fear—royal blood was shed,
but the royal assassins are not yet dead.

SECOND CHORISTER

That, my child, is the best wish you could make,
better than gold. But making that wish come true   330
is not so easy. Your father will not rest
if you stand here mourning, beating your head and breast,
while, there in the palace, our masters laugh at you.
It is a dreadful thing!
You two are the children of a king.
Let them beware of every step you take.

ORESTES

Those words are true. They pierce the ground
like arrows, and hit their mark below—

my father's ear,
and heart, and, by their muffled sound,   340
he is comforted to know
what we plan here.
Zeus, send up from those spirits that passion
we need, to act in the reckless and desperate fashion
these bloody deeds will demand.
Retribution is at hand.

SECOND CHORISTER

    I cannot wait.
I rejoice—I admit it—that it may be my fate
to watch and approve and to cheer
when I see that bad man hacked to pieces here,   350
or else be transfixed with a sword
that pierces the lady who lies beneath her lord.
When both of them have died
as they deserve, of course
in agony and remorse,
I shall be satisfied.

ELECTRA

    It will be grand,
and the deed will be done by Zeus' powerful hand.
They'll be our pair of sacrificial goats,
and for our rite   360
we'll slash their outstretched miserable throats
and then watch the bright
blood gush onto the polished marble floor.
They deserve this, and more.

FIRST CHORISTER

    This is the only way.
This is what all the priests and prophets say,
that blood is requited by blood,
and evil must be made good.

Our mighty king is dead,
and ruin must follow—on Clytemnestra's head.   370

ORESTES

You mighty powers of hell, behold me now
and do not curse me. Give me, instead, your blessing
and your strength, which I shall use, I vow,
in a just cause. Your wrongs deserve redressing.

SECOND CHORISTER

I am torn between grief and hope as I hear
these piteous words. The child has lost
his father, and his own life, too, which is worthless now—
except as an instrument of heavenly vengeance
at whatever cost.

ELECTRA

Anger and grief are our parents now, and pain   380
is the god to whom we pray. We are become
wild children wolves have reared, with a human brain,
but the heart of a beast, implacable and dumb.

CHORUS

Like Asiatic women, we wail,
ululate in our hurt, and cry,
"Suffer, suffer, suffer." We claw our faces,
smite our breasts, and call out, over and over,
"Suffer and die!"

ELECTRA

Die, Mother, a death painful and slow,
and, mourned by no one at all, you, too, shall know   390
what it is to be laid in the earth without a tear
that anyone sheds on your deserted bier.

ORESTES

What words are these for children to say? What shame
we feel, though we are not to blame.
Either with the god's help, or all alone,
I will put matters right and make her atone
for what she did, our mother and his wife.
Let me kill her, and then end my own life.

FIRST CHORISTER

Oh, Agamemnon, the horror of it. They
mutilated your corpse. We saw them hack   400
your arms off in the barbarous way
that's done to murderers, to keep them from coming back
as ghosts to menace their executioners. Sleep,
knowing your children are here together to weep,
and that they are prepared to do
what they know you would want them to.

ELECTRA

It was as they say. Horrid and vile. They did
these things to him, and then together hid
me in my room like a vicious dog in a pen
where I could curse and cry in my rage and then   410
subside to bitter tears. What else could I do
but weep and pray and wait, dear brother, for you?

SECOND CHORISTER

Hear her, remember what she says, and carry
the weight of her words like ballast to steady your soul.
Thus moved, you cannot be deflected as anger
drives you, single-minded, toward your goal.

ORESTES

Father, help us. Intercede for your children.

ELECTRA

In tears, I also plead. Father, help us.

FIRST CHORISTER

To this, your prayer, we add our fervent "amen."
Hear them! Emerge from the darkness as spirits sometimes   420
are able to do to aid in a pious cause.

ORESTES

It is war, and each side prays to Ares for aid,
and each side calls upon Justice. Hear our cry!

ELECTRA

The gods see all, know all, and will judge the right.

FIRST CHORISTER

I shudder to hear this.
What we have long supposed,
imagined, expected, even assumed,
is happening now, but differently, out of control.

We understand it is not our imagination
but that of the gods that controls events now. Trouble,   430
born in blood, inherited in the blood,
has been waiting all these years. And Até—ruin—
swoops down like a bird of prey on this house.

Sorrow, sorrow on sorrow inconsolable,
and a throbbing pain that cannot be assuaged.
If there be cure, it must come from within these walls.
Desperate remedies, drastic measures—blood,
flowing through time in powerful tides. Oh, gods,
and you, the blessed dead, protect us, help us,
help these children sent forth into a world   440
of evil and peril and woe.
All of you down below,
be with them as they go.

ORESTES

> Father, you died an inglorious, un-royal death.
> Hear my prayer! I dedicate life and breath
> to righting the wrong you suffered. I come to claim
> your throne and clear the family's sullied name.

ELECTRA

> And I have a prayer beyond what Orestes has said—
> that we escape with our lives when Aegisthus is dead.

ORESTES

> Yes, and we'll have a funeral feast, a great   450
> wake in your honor, Father. As there should have been
> long ago, with the burnt offerings you
> deserved but never had. This was a sin
> for which we shall make atonement with what we do.

ELECTRA

> I dream that, on the day of my wedding feast,
> we shall also pour libations in your name.
> I take my oath. The father of a bride
> deserves honor, and you shall have then the same
> reverence we do you now at your graveside.

ORESTES

> Earth! Earth, lie lightly upon him. Open   460
> and let him ascend to watch and aid my combat.

ELECTRA

> Persephone, hear us, and grant that we may triumph!

ORESTES

> Think of it! In a bathtub! Oh, Father!

ELECTRA

> Like a snared animal, helpless!

ORESTES
> Trussed, and not by her but by Fate itself!

ELECTRA
> But the shame and the blame are hers!

ORESTES
> O Father, how can you bear it? How can we?

ELECTRA
> Help us! Raise your head from its cold pillow . . .

ORESTES
> Send Diké to help us. Let us take hold
> of their throats as they took hold of yours. Give us   470
> that satisfaction they took in killing you!

ELECTRA
> Father, your fledgling chicks are perched here singing
> here at your tomb. Hear us and have compassion
> on him and on me.
> Here in the Peloponnese, let the line of Pelops
> continue. Let us live and thrive and have issue.
> Through us, you will be
> immortal, as men can be, almost like gods.
> Even the dead can hope. Drowned men can rise
> like corks in the sea,   480
> and corpses ascend from their graves to thrive
> and prosper in air, in their heirs who are yet alive.
> Grant us our plea.

FIRST CHORISTER
> Splendid words, but words are easy enough.
> It feels good to stand here, complain, and threaten,
> and pray to the gods and the dead. But the time soon comes
> to turn from words and prayers to the world of action.

ORESTES

It shall be so. But let us proceed with care.
I must know the lay of the land. How does it happen
that she has ordered or even allowed these libations?   490
A sudden change of heart? Some pang of remorse?
If so, why is she not here herself? These rites
are at once too grand and altogether too mean
to make any sense to me. If she felt what she should,
she'd have come here alone, I'd think, and killed herself.

FIRST CHORISTER

That, I can answer, young man. I was there and saw it
and heard it all. She had a dream, a nightmare,
and woke up in terror. She sent, therefore, these women . . .
The godless will sometimes ask for believers' prayers.

ORESTES

Did she say what she had dreamt?   500

FIRST CHORISTER

She did, indeed. She had given birth to a dragon.

ORESTES

Was that the whole thing? What happened after that?

FIRST CHORISTER

She laid her monster baby in swaddling clothes.

ORESTES

I see. And what did she feed it?

FIRST CHORISTER

She gave it suck, from her own breast.

ORESTES

And it bit her nipple?

FIRST CHORISTER

Exactly, and sucked her blood along with her milk.

ORESTES

Some dreams are riddles. This one is clear enough.

FIRST CHORISTER

And then she woke, shrieking in fear, appalled,
and ordered the lamps be lit. She walked the floors,   510
and sent these women here to the burial ground
to perform the rites for the dead and pour libations.
It was all she could think of to do, in her great distress.

ORESTES

A lovely dream. A prophetic dream, I pray,
and I call on the gods and my father's ghost to fulfill it.
That dragon comes from the same womb as I, and lay
in the same cradle, bound in those swaddling clothes,
and it opened its mouth to suck at the very breast
that nourished me. If blood mixed with the milk,
and she recoiled in terror, it is all her doing.   520
The portent is clear—death by violence, and I,
that child whom she turned to a dragon, I shall kill her.

FIRST CHORISTER

It is hard to argue with that. I hope you are right.
What can we do to help? Or at least not hinder?

ORESTES

It's more or less straightforward. My sister goes in
and she—and you—will say nothing, not a word.
By trickery they killed my father; deceit
is not inappropriate now. Apollo himself,
the god of truth, commands us all to dissemble.
    I shall appear as an alien. We shall appear,   530
Pylades and I, as guests and allies

We'll speak with the accent of Phocis, and claim we come
from Parnassus' slopes. They will receive us well,
as a house in trouble must do. They would otherwise fear
to be seen to be fearful. In the absence of truth and law,
appearance is all they have. They will let us in.
    They will usher us, then, to the throne-room, and there,
          on the throne
my father used to sit on, I'll see Aegisthus,
and he shall see me . . . And recognize me? Perhaps.
But by then it will be too late, for with my sharp sword   540
I'll cleave his villainous head like a log for stove-wood.
And the Erinyes shall have their third round of drinks,
blood, as red as claret, and drunk down hot
as it spurts, fresh and delicious, out of the wineskin.
    You, Electra, will watch what goes on and warn me
if anything suddenly changes. And you, good women,
you will oblige me simply by keeping silent.
For the rest, we are in the hands of the god Apollo,
by whose great grace I have managed to come this far.
I pray he may let me continue on to the end   550
and guide this hand that holds my avenging sword.
(Orestes, Pylades, and Electra exit.)

FIRST CHORISTER
    The earth is full of horrors,
    and the sea, too,
    monsters, teeming as in a nightmare,
    the creatures we somehow deserve.
    They are waiting to spring.
    Even the skies are full of menace—stars
    fall to earth in dreadful portent. Where
    can we run? There are birds of prey, enormous insects
    whirling about our heads, and crawly vermin   560
    on every side where we pick our way in disgust.
    And a storm is coming up. On our faces
    we feel the first gust.

SECOND CHORISTER

    What can we say of men
    who are driven insane?
    And what about women who go quite mad,
    turn hard and mean in their souls?
    Passion can do such a thing.
    In marriage there ought to be some safety,
    but nothing is ever secure, and love can go bad   570
    in a moment, and husbands and wives will look at each other
    in utter loathing. And parents will come to despise their children
    as Althaea, Meleagar's mother, grew to hate
    her son—and she threw his life's log
    onto that burning grate.

FIRST CHORISTER

    And I know another tale,
    of Nisus' daughter Scylla, who fell in love
    with Minos, the king of Crete.
    For a golden necklace that Minos gave her, a small
    gift, she was smitten. And forthwith she betrayed   580
    her father, her city, her people, all
    for love. She cut off Nisus' lock of purple hairs
    that had protected him, and Hermes, Hades' usher,
    came to take him away to the land of shades.

SECOND CHORISTER

    Those wives of Lemnos, too,
    jealous of their husbands' Thracian slaves,
    murdered them, every one.
    Later, when Jason came to their island, he found
    only women. There is no limit whatever
    to the evil they'll do. He looked around,   590
    and not a male had survived. Their race
    died out, of course. Rejected by gods and hated
    by nature, too, they disappeared forever.

FIRST CHORISTER

    It happens that way. Men and women sin,
    as if, overhead, there were no sword of Justice,
    its edge sharp enough that no small gleam of light
    glinted off it, to remind us to do right.

SECOND CHORISTER

    That sword is forged on Destiny's huge anvil,
    and Justice waits with the Erinyes to cure
    corruption. She has sent to this house its son   600
    to put right evil things that have been done.
(The scene shifts to the palace gate. Orestes, Pylades, and their attendants
enter. Orestes knocks at the gate.)

ORESTES

    Hello? Hello in there! Doorman! Hello?
    Is anyone home? Can anyone hear me knocking?
    For the fourth time, hello! Is this the house
    of Aegisthus? Does it offer welcome to strangers?
(A servant appears.)

SERVANT

    I hear you! I'm coming, coming . . . Hold on there, stranger.
    Greetings. And now, who are you? And where do you
            come from?

ORESTES

    Announce me, if you would, to your masters. I come
    with news for them, from far away. I have traveled
    long, and night is coming on. It's time   610
    to rest. Let someone in charge know that I'm here.
    Tell your mistress, or better, tell your master,
    for I have news and wish to tell it plainly

without polite palaver. A man can talk
to another man in a clear and straightforward way.
(*The servant withdraws. A moment later, Clytemnestra appears with a
female servant in attendance.*)

CLYTEMNESTRA
You are welcome, gentlemen. Whatever you may need,
don't hesitate to ask. We have food and drink,
warm baths, soft beds, and eager attendants to serve you.
If you have some important news to impart
to the master of the house, I shall fetch him for you.   620

ORESTES
I am a stranger, a Daulian from Phocis,
and I come to Argos on certain private business.
Along the way, at an inn, I met a man,
a traveler on the road, who was also from Phocis.
Strophius was his name. We got to talking,
and he told me that, if I was going on to Argos,
I ought to visit here and deliver the message
to the parents of Orestes—to let them know
their son is dead. I regret bringing such news,
but I am charged to ask his parents' wishes: 630
should his friends bury his ashes where he died,
or should they return them here to his birthplace?
I have no idea to whom I should put these questions,
you or another. If you could introduce me . . .

CLYTEMNESTRA (*shaking her head*)
Ah, me! Me. And your tale is my undoing.
This house is cursed, and the taint is everywhere . . .
Even Orestes, out of harm's way, I had thought . . .
But the aim of the Fates is deadly at any distance.

We had hoped he might be spared . . . and his sister, too,
had prayed for his return. She'll take it hard.   640
Her celebration will never happen now.

ORESTES

I should have preferred to come to a house like this
with better news. Those ties of guest and host
that the gods hold dear are strained by such sad tidings.
But what else could I do? I had given my promise . . .

CLYTEMNESTRA

Rest assured, your welcome shall be as warm
as if you had brought us news we were pleased to hear.
It wasn't your doing. And if not you, then another
would have pronounced those words you have just spoken.
But you must be exhausted. And tired and thirsty.   650
Come inside.
(to an attendant)
                    Take them to the guest quarters, him, his friend,
and their attendants, and give them whatever they want,
as befits our house. You know what to do. Meanwhile,
I shall convey your sad news to my lord
and we shall, no doubt, consult with our friends and advisors.
(All exit, except the chorus.)

FIRST CHORISTER

Knowing what we know, it is hard to keep still,
as we hear her talk that way to her son Orestes.
Not to laugh or cry out . . .

SECOND CHORISTER

It is hard for the earth herself not to laugh aloud,
and hard, I am sure, for the tomb of the king to keep silent   660
and not call out in protest or sheer derision.

FIRST CHORISTER

This is no time for blurting out what we think.
This is the hour of subtle persuasion and guile.

SECOND CHORISTER

This is the time when Hermes comes forth from the shadows
to work by craft and stealth the will of the gods.
(*Orestes' nurse Cilissa enters.*)

FIRST CHORISTER

What's going on inside? Is it going well?
I see Orestes' nurse, Cilissa, in tears.
What can that mean? Tell us, why do you weep?

CILISSA

My mistress has sent me in haste to summon Aegisthus
to interrogate the guest about his story.   670
She pretends to grief, but the servants can see in her eyes
that joy she tries to hide and relief as well.
It's bad for this house, ruin. Our last real hope
is gone. And Aegisthus will exult to hear
the news it breaks my heart to have to tell him.
These tears on my face are real enough. I have seen
troubles, ancient griefs that beget new griefs,
but nothing so bad as this. What happened to them
was very bad, but this was my little Orestes,
the boy I nursed at my breast. I held him at night   680
when he had colic, or bad dreams, or fevers.
I soothed his infant wailing, knowing well
what cause he could not know about for crying.
A tiny, innocent creature, I fed him and held him
and wiped his little ass and washed his diapers . . .
This was the baby Agamemnon gave me
to care for and love, and I did, as well as I could.
I loved him so . . . And now I must go to Aegisthus,

the bane of this house, to tell him Orestes is dead,
and see his great delight, and stand there mute.   690

SECOND CHORISTER
But what did she say, exactly? How should he come?

CILISSA
She said that he should come right away. What else?

FIRST CHORISTER
Exactly! What else? Was he to come armed and attended?

CILISSA
Yes, with his guards.

FIRST CHORISTER
                                          But you will amend that message.
Garble it some, or even try to correct it.
Tell him to come alone. It's such good news,
he has no need of his guards. Why cause him worry?
Believe me, it's better this way. It's a twisted message,
but we can straighten it out. Do you take my meaning?

CILISSA
Frankly, no. Why are you glad? What is this?   700

FIRST CHORISTER
It could be good that the gods intend for us.

CILISSA
                                                             How?
Orestes is dead! Didn't you hear what I said?

SECOND CHORISTER
She thinks he's dead, but perhaps she could be mistaken.

CILISSA
> Isn't he dead? Do you know something I don't?

FIRST CHORISTER
> You don't want to ask. Go and deliver your message.
> Don't give up hope. Trust us, and trust in the gods.

CILISSA
> I'll do as you say. And pray that it turns out well.
> *(Cilissa exits.)*

FIRST CHORISTER
> O Zeus, Zeus, father of gods,
> grant us a good outcome, here in this house,
> that order should rule, and Justice prevail, and good.   710
> In abject reverence, we pray
> that those who succeed are those who should.
> You have sent him here, O Zeus.
> Grant him your protection, here in this house,
> and bless his efforts. He will repay you with prayer
> to which we shall add our "amen,"
> for he is the city's savior and rightful heir.

SECOND CHORISTER
> That noble steed you loved is gone,
> but this is his foal, his colt. Protect him, Zeus,
> hitched as he is in Destiny's traces.   720
> Go light with the whip. Rely
> on his spirit, his heart, his excellent breeding,
> and the fire that gleams in his eye.

> And you, Apollo, in your Delphic cave,
> look in a kindly way on this wretched house.
> Clear the miasma of guilt and sin, and allow
> fresh air into these high walls.

Freedom and Justice are more than empty dreams
or memories in these halls.

FIRST CHORISTER

Hermes, Maia's son, give him your aid,   730
with eloquence, guile, whatever he may require.
Contrive by your darkness a restoration of light.
Lies can lead to the truth.
We do what we have to do. Forgive us, gods,
and help this good youth.

CHORUS

Then, in gladness, shall we sing together here,
that the wind blows fair and the ship has righted itself.
The storm is past. The ocean is calm, and the sky
is blue. Who can remember the force of the tempest,
and the winds' relentless and desolating cry?   740

FIRST CHORISTER

There will come, gods willing, a moment of recognition
when all is made plain at last and stark and clear,
when he calls out in rage and anguish, "My father!"
and she looks about for help and, finding none,
sees him approach and calls out in her terror, "My son."

SECOND CHORISTER

The days of heroes are not yet over. This one
comes to fight monsters as fierce as that sea-dragon
Perseus slew. But these, more horrid, resemble
his own kin. Let him not flinch from the deed
but strike, and again. For their bloodshed they must bleed.   750

(*Aegisthus enters.*)

AEGISTHUS

They sent for me! This is bad news, bad news . . .
Orestes is dead, they tell me. A terrible thing.

It's hard to bear, one loss after another,
but what can you do? We have to go on somehow.
I'll talk to the man. Maybe it isn't true.
A rumor, or some washerwomen's gossip . . .
Have any of you any actual information?

FIRST CHORISTER
We have heard what you've heard. The man is inside,
the stranger who brought the news. You can ask him yourself.

AEGISTHUS
I'll do that. Right away. I'll ask him questions   760
and see what he has to say for himself. Did he see it,
or only hear about it at second hand?
I'll find out the truth soon enough, you can bet on that.
(Aegisthus exits.)

SECOND CHORISTER
What can we say? How do we dare frame
a prayer to Zeus? The sword is out of its sheath
and, one way or another, will now draw blood.
Is this the end of the royal house? Or the start
of something new and better? I hold my breath
and hope for the best, that Orestes may play his part
well, and regain the power and wealth that are his,   770
restoring justice, and vindicating his name.

FIRST CHORISTER
How do we bear the waiting? What can we do . . . ?
(A shriek is heard from inside the palace.)

AEGISTHUS *(from inside)*
Oooh! Oh, god! Oh, god . . .

FIRST CHORISTER
That's it. Whatever it is, it is happening now.

SECOND CHORISTER
> You were asking, "What can we do?"

FIRST CHORISTER
> The answer, for the moment at least, is obvious.
> We do and say as little as possible. We stand here and wait
> to hear what has happened. We'll keep out of the way.
> When we hear who is still alive, we'll know how to behave.
> *(First Chorister leads the way off to the extreme edge of stage right.*
> > *A servant of Aegisthus comes rushing in from*
> > *stage left.)*

SERVANT
> Oh, heaven! Woe! Woe! My master is dead.   780
> Lord, lord, lord . . . Aegisthus is slain.
> Help, somebody! Not for him. But the killer
> is still in there, and who knows what he'll do next?
> Call Clytemnestra . . . What are you standing there for?
> Are you deaf? Or paralyzed? Or stupid? What?
> Somebody warn the queen! Call out the guards . . .
> *(Clytemnestra hurries onstage.)*

CLYTEMNESTRA
> What's all this noise? What's going on? You there . . .

SERVANT
> The dead are killing the living. And vice versa . . .

CLYTEMNESTRA
> You're making riddles. But what you mean is plain.
> It looks to be payback time. Fetch me a weapon,   790
> a battle-axe from the wall. Hurry. Go!
> Win or lose, it won't be without a fight.
> *(Servant exits. The inner door is opened and the corpse of Aegisthus is*
> > *revealed with Orestes standing over it. Pylades*
> > *is nearby.)*

ORESTES
(to Clytemnestra)
    You are the one I'm looking for. I'm done with him.

CLYTEMNESTRA
    Aegisthus? Dead? Oh, my beloved . . .

ORESTES
                                        Him?
    You loved that man? Then you won't be sorry to join him
    in death, and in the same damned grave, together.

CLYTEMNESTRA
    Wait, my son. Have pity. I am your mother.
    I nursed you at these breasts when you were a baby!
    How can you turn against me now?

ORESTES
                                        Pity?
    Pylades, what shall I do? She is my mother!   800

PYLADES
    What did Apollo command you to do? You gave
    your oath, remember? Can you offend the gods
    and all mankind as well?

ORESTES
                            You are right, my friend.
(to Clytemnestra)
    With him, then. You preferred him to my father?
    You chose him over honor and those vows
    you took as my father's bride, all of them lies?
    Now you can lie with him, undisturbed, forever.

CLYTEMNESTRA
    You don't have to do this. Let me live out my years . . .

ORESTES
As the Queen Mother? You, who killed the king?

CLYTEMNESTRA
It's Fate you must blame, my child.

ORESTES
As you can, too.   810
You can blame Fate for your death instead of me.

CLYTEMNESTRA
Have you no fear of a mother's curse?

ORESTES
No,
not if you've done your worst to me already.
You sent me away into exile.

CLYTEMNESTRA
No, into safety!
I sent you away to the house of a friend and ally.

ORESTES
An ally, but I was sent as a slave and a hostage.

CLYTEMNESTRA
It's not true.

ORESTES
Mother, it happened to me.
I was there. I know what happened.

CLYTEMNESTRA
You know
what your father did! Where is your anger for him?

ORESTES

He was away at war. You were at home,   820
safe in your bed.

CLYTEMNESTRA

And all alone. And abandoned.

ORESTES

That happens when men go to war.

CLYTEMNESTRA

Orestes,
listen to me. I am your mother.

ORESTES

I know.
And you have brought us to this. This is your doing.

CLYTEMNESTRA

The hounds of hell will avenge a mother's murder.

ORESTES

The hounds of hell are my old friends. They require
that I avenge my father's bloody murder.

CLYTEMNESTRA

Talking to you is like talking to a stone.

ORESTES

A gravestone, say. What's written there can't change.

CLYTEMNESTRA

This is that nightmare dragon I bore and suckled.   830

ORESTES

> That was a dream of truth. You killed your husband,
> a vile and impossible deed. It demands another,
> at least as outrageous and vile.
> *(He forces Clytemnestra inside, behind the inner curtain.*
> *Pylades follows.)*

FIRST CHORISTER

> I feel a double sorrow. The house
> was attacked by a pair of beasts, and now
> their depredations are done. But at what great cost!
> The exile has returned, and his father's ghost
> may rest in peace below,
> his honor restored, as king, parent, and spouse.

SECOND CHORISTER

> For the sins against us of Priam's sons,   840
> Justice exacted a retribution
> of wealth and blood. And here, at home, it's the same
> closing out of accounts, for the guilt and its shame.
> Now, for the dire pollution
> of the marriage bed, payment is due at once.

FIRST CHORISTER

> The name of Justice is no mere abstraction.
> The true daughter of Zeus, she corrects those who
> transgress, defacing the cosmos by their action.
> We recognize her chastisements as true
> and necessary. Her world *just is*, we may say.   850
> With all that is not just, she does away.

SECOND CHORISTER

> Let us rejoice in our deliverance, praise
> Apollo and Zeus, and thank the Fates. The days
> of misery and disgrace are done, and we

may serve the gods in pride and decency. Time
passes, and somehow cleanses unspeakable crime.
This is the day we hoped we would live to see.
(*The inner curtain opens, revealing Orestes with a suppliant's wreath
                    and an olive branch standing by the bodies of
                    Clytemnestra and Aegisthus. With him are Pylades
                    and a couple of attendants who display the robe
                    of Agamemnon.*)

ORESTES
    Here they are, these two. They killed my father,
    plundered the wealth of the house, and seized its power.
    They did it, they said, out of love that bound them together.   860
    They are bound together now, in the infernal union
    of guilt and death. It's what they deserved and demanded.
    Look at that robe, that accursed garment. They used it
    to cover my father and tangle him up. And they kept it,
    a memento, a trophy. Or, say, the people's exhibit.
    Spread it out! Let the citizens look in horror
    at what they did. The father of all things, the Sun,
    Apollo, whose eye sees everywhere, was the witness.
    The rest of us now can stare in amazed disgust
    at what they did. The hero's hands and feet   870
    were wrapped in this gaudy rag, as they struck and struck,
    again and again. No one can say I did this—
    killed my own mother—without good cause.
    As far as he is concerned, no cause was required.
    He is not worth discussing. He had committed
    adultery, and the law is clear, and he suffered
    the penalty it prescribes. But she, my mother . . .
    She was a monster and should have been born a viper,
    or dragon, or some such creature men know to fear
    for their poisonous exhalations, a touch or a look   880
    that at once corrupts with shamelessness and evil.
(*He takes the bloody robe from the attendants.*)
    And what is this? A trap for a beast? A shroud?

It is a rag, a sorry piece of goods.
This was the wool they pulled over his eyes.
A horrible thing! Sheep's clothing those wolves,
cowardly, covered him with, when they stabbed him to death.
There are no limits to what a woman will do.
May the gods protect me from such as her. To marry
is to put your life into somebody else's hands.
(He drops the robe.)

FIRST CHORISTER
Terrible, terrible. A dreadful death for her,   890
and an all but unbearable life for him, her son.

ORESTES
She did it herself. Look at that bloody garment
with the holes the sword tore through its elegant work,
but the blood of a king is a very expensive dye.
(to the attendants)
Take it away. Now I can say my prayers
at my father's tomb and grieve for him, undistracted
by the anger I felt. Instead, there now is guilt,
but I shall contrive somehow to live with that.
(The attendants exit with the robe.)

SECOND CHORISTER
Nothing in life is pure. There is guilt and pain
in whatever we do, from the first day to the last,   900
hour by hour and even breath by breath.

ORESTES
True enough, as a general rule. But for this,
there are, I think, no rules. For what I suffer,
there is no recommended therapy or treatment.
What I feel is . . . giddy, with joy and horror dancing together.
My ears are alive with the roar of my own heartbeat,
and it's hard to speak, or breathe, or even think . . .

But the one thought I cling to is that what I did
was necessary and right. She killed my father,
betrayed him and killed him. An affront to gods and men,   910
it had to be put right. And I have done that.
    What happens to me now? Apollo promised
it would be all right. I would not be adjudged as guilty
of matricide. But rather, if I did nothing,
if I failed to act, then I should share in the evil,
and suffer unimaginably and forever.
    I hold out this suppliant's wreath, and the olive branch,
and I go to Delphi to pray at the sacred altar
before its eternal flame, as the god instructed,
to pray for exoneration and men's forgiveness.   920
I charge you, people of Argos, to bear witness to this
as I go forth, a wanderer now and a stranger,
leaving my home again on this pious quest.

FIRST CHORISTER

You have done well, and again you behave correctly.
You need say nothing further. What teems in your brain
we can barely imagine. But we wish you well.
You have freed Argos from this two-headed beast.

ORESTES

I have. And there they are. Like a couple of Gorgons,
horrible, horrible. I can't look anymore.

SECOND CHORISTER

Spare yourself. It hasn't been easy. Your father   930
would surely approve. Think only of him.

ORESTES

And those hounds of hell my mother spoke of, baying
and belling? What do I do to get free of them?

FIRST CHORISTER

> It's the blood still fresh on your hands. You can wash that away.
> Give yourself a little time to recover.

ORESTES

> And all that time I shall hear those baying dogs,
> slobbering blood and rolling their savage eyes.

SECOND CHORISTER

> Apollo will exorcise these distressing phantoms
> and heal your troubled spirit.

ORESTES

>   Phantoms?
> They are real. I see them, as clearly as I see you.   940
> They hunger for my blood. I must get away.

(He rushes off.)

SECOND CHORISTER

> Our blessings go with you. May the gods keep you safe
>   from harm
> and, after what you have been through, give you peace.

FIRST CHORISTER

> Three times that fever has come upon this house.
> Thyestes' children first, then Agamemnon,
> stabbed in his bath, and now these murders,
> a penance, or a deliverance . . . Who can say?

SECOND CHORISTER

> When will the plan of the gods be carried out?
> Only then will the fury be lulled and the suffering stop.